A GUIDE TO THE KITCHEN QUADRANT

A GUIDE TO THE KITCHEN QUADRANT

THE UNOFFICIAL *FOURTH WING* COOKBOOK

CHELSEA COLE

weldonowen

FOR MOLLY.

Written while you fluttered under my ribs, the calm before the flight.

CONTENTS

STRATEGIC ACCOMPANIMENTS

SWEETS AND SMALL INDULGENCES

HEALING TINCTURES AND SPIRITED CONCOCTIONS

MENUS FOR MAYHEM AND MERRIMENT

A NOTE FROM THE AUTHOR

DEAR FELLOW WANNABE RIDERS,

Welcome to *A Guide to the Kitchen Quadrant*, a culinary tribute to the world of The Empyrean: a series that swept me off my feet faster than a wyvern attack and hasn't let me down since. This collection of recipes is inspired by the foods, characters, and moments that have made *Fourth Wing*, *Iron Flame*, and *Onyx Storm* such a deliciously wild ride.

I wasn't looking for a new obsession when I picked up *Fourth Wing*. Honestly, I was looking for something to cure my book hangover from that other wildly popular series. What I got was a world full of dragons, rebels, heartache, and a heroine whose voice felt instantly familiar. I devoured the books (a few times, if we're being honest), then started dreaming up what might be on the table in Basgiath's mess hall between training sessions.

Some of these recipes are directly inspired by dishes mentioned in the books. (Yes, Xaden's Chocolate Cake is in here—page 110). Others are born from characters, places, or just the general chaos of being a cadet at Basgiath War College. They're meant to be practical and comforting, but never boring. Things our favorite riders would be excited to reach for again and again.

This cookbook is for everyone, whether you're a kitchen cadet or a culinary wingleader. I've designed these recipes to be approachable, customizable, and, most importantly, fun. I hope you'll use this book not only for everyday meals, but also for book clubs, themed parties, or a watch party (IYKYK).

A quick warning: This book contains spoilers for The Empyrean books one through three. If you haven't finished *Onyx Storm*, proceed with caution, or just embrace the chaos, like a true rider.

Creating this book while pregnant with my daughter, Molly, and alongside my one-year-old son, Reggie, made this whole experience feel even more meaningful. Even though she wasn't yet here, she lived through months of recipe development, rewrites, and late-night brainstorms, just as her brother had done twice before her. If they grow up half as brave as Violet Sorrengail, I'll consider it a win.

From my kitchen to yours: May your spices be strong, your knives be sharp, and your squad always have your back.

Until the last venin falls—

CHELSEA COLE

FROM THE BOOK OF BRENNAN

YOUR GUIDE TO THE GUIDE

Fragment recovered from the personal effects of Cadet Violet Sorrengail.
Annotation and confirmation by Jesinia of the Scribe Quadrant.

To the Reader,

If you're reading this, congratulations: You're still breathing.

You've crossed the Parapet. Maybe you've lived through Threshing, the Gauntlet, betrayal, heartbreak, victory, loss. Maybe you're covered in scars. Maybe you're just hungry.

Whatever the reason, I'm not here to lecture you. Gods know you've had enough of that from your dragon, I'm sure.

This isn't a rule book. It's not a codex. It's something to get you through when your squad's running on fumes and the mess hall is half ash. These are meals for people who've fought for their lives and then had to fight again before dessert.

So eat. Share if you can. Hide the last roll if you must. And if you burn the first batch, that just means you're trying. Keep at it.

YOU'VE GOT TO EAT SOMETHING

This guide is broken up the way your day usually is, if you're lucky:

- A Rider's Breakfast for early mornings and high stakes
- Study Snacks Fit for a Scribe because staying awake through Battle Brief is a battle of its own
- Midday Fuel to keep you on your feet when the aches set in
- Feasts After Flight for the rare nights when you have something to celebrate
- Strategic Accompaniments for meals that need backup
- Sweets and Small Indulgences because sometimes dessert is the win
- Healing Tinctures and Spirited Concoctions for recovery, revenge, or whatever comes next

Some of these recipes are based on things actually served in Navarre. Some are guesses. A few are what I wish had been on the table back then. All are made to get you through the kind of day where you dodge flame before breakfast and death before bed.

THIS BOOK IS FOR FIRST YEARS

No one's born knowing how to fly, or cook, for that matter. You don't have to be fancy. You just have to try.

These recipes don't assume you've got elite-level skills or a kitchen the size of the Archives. They're written for real people. Hungry ones. The kind who might still be wearing sparring leathers while they're whisking a sauce.

You'll screw up a few things. You'll get better. That's how it works.

STOCK THE ARMORY

If you're going to learn to cook, you need supplies. Just like battle.

These are the ingredients that show up again and again in this guide because they get the job done. Think of them as the standard-issue gear of your kitchen. Keep these on hand and you'll be ready to throw together a feast, a recovery meal, or a quick snack before you run out the door for patrol.

And no, this isn't a full inventory. Use your judgment (assuming you have some).

OILS AND FATS

- Extra-virgin olive oil (yes, the good kind)
- Mayonnaise

SUGARS AND SWEETENERS

- Brown sugar
- Granulated sugar
- Honey
- Powdered sugar

FLOURS AND GRAINS

- All-purpose flour
- Panko or dried bread crumbs (for maximum crunch in minimal time)
- Rolled oats

SPICES AND SEASONINGS

- Black pepper
- Dried oregano
- Garlic powder
- Ground cinnamon
- Ground ginger
- Kosher salt (not the iodized stuff unless you want your food to taste like regret)
- Red pepper flakes (for those who flirt with danger and flavor)
- Smoked paprika

HERBS AND CITRUS

- Fresh cilantro
- Fresh dill
- Fresh parsley
- Fresh rosemary
- Lemons

DAIRY

- Cream cheese
- Eggs
- Feta cheese
- Greek yogurt
- Heavy cream
- Unsalted butter
- Whole milk

PANTRY EXTRAS

- Canned chickpeas
- Canned diced tomatoes
- Chicken or vegetable broth
- Chocolate chips
- Peanut butter
- Tomato paste

BAR ESSENTIALS (THE GOOD STUFF)

- Bitters
- Bourbon
- Empress 1908 gin
- Vodka

You don't need all of this to start. But if your shelves are stocked and your blades are sharp, you'll be ready for anything. Even if "anything" turns out to be brunch for six and a dragon with opinions.

Bored on patrol duty? Spotting mushrooms instead of venin? Pocket 'em. Fonilee berries, wild herbs, anything that grows and is edible—they'll come in handy later. Just maybe double-check they're not poisonous before tossing them in a stew. We've lost enough riders to actual battle.

GEAR UP

Don't panic if you don't have everything. Here's what helps:

- A bench scraper
- A Dutch oven (versatile and indestructible—just like you)
- Candy thermometer
- Edible pearlescent powder (for when your food needs to be the distraction)
- Fine-mesh sieve
- Muffin pans
- Parchment paper (precut = smart, not weak)
- Rimmed baking sheets
- Stand mixer (optional); hand mixer (plenty)
- Wire cooling racks
- Zester (fine-rasp grater)

Use what you've got. Make it work. That's the point.

NOTES IN THE MARGINS

Jesinia's notes are scattered throughout this book. Don't ignore them. She's smarter than most of us and ten times as generous.

If she tells you to reduce the sauce or to take the shortcut, listen.

If she sounds like she's preemptively scolding Violet for skipping a step, she probably is.

But she wouldn't have written any of it if she didn't care.

EAT TOGETHER WHEN YOU CAN

Near the end of this book, you'll find a stash of menus—meals meant to be shared.

They're built for book clubs that turn into battle debriefs, for formal dinners where alliances are formed over second helpings, and for brunches where the dress code is "leathers optional."

Whether you're hosting a feast worthy of the rebellion, throwing a Gauntlet Eve carbo load, or just gathering your squad to scream about cliffhangers, these menus are here to help you plan the kind of meal that turns into a memory.

Pick one. Make it your own. Just make sure there's enough for seconds.

We do not eat our allies. Unless they double-dip in the sauce. Then, it's a judgment call.

—TAIRN

Brown dragons do not tolerate fear. Neither does an empty stomach.

1

A RIDER'S BREAKFAST

There's a misguided belief that the most dangerous time of day for a cadet is during combat training or flight maneuvers. It's not. It's breakfast. Half the quadrant is hungover, three-quarters are armed, and the rest are still deciding if today is the day they kill someone for using the last of the jam.

—Major Afendra's Guide to the Riders Quadrant
(Unauthorized Edition)

Mornings at Basgiath wait for no one, not even dragons. This chapter is a tribute to the crack-of-dawn chaos that defines life in the Riders Quadrant: the bark of a wingleader, the sting of cold air on the flight field, and the desperate need to eat something—anything—before the first round of drills. Whether you're scarfing down a sandwich while dodging flames, poisoning a pastry with precision, or grabbing a handful of granola before a run, these recipes were built for speed, sustenance, and the kind of riders who survive—not in spite of the odds but because of them.

Fuel up. You're going to need it.

YIELDS 8 SERVINGS

WINGLEADER'S WAKE-UP QUICHE

Eggs and sausage show up at nearly every Basgiath breakfast for good reason: Nothing prepares a rider for flight drills, survival courses, or sparring matches like a serious hit of protein. This quiche folds those eggs and sausage into a golden, flaky crust with cubes of sharp cheddar and just enough attitude to get you through the morning. Even better? It reheats like a dream, which is a necessity when hot meals are a luxury. And if you're dragging after a night of, say, particularly vigorous signet usage, don't worry. As a certain dragon once offered, "Shall I get the Wingleader?" . . . to reheat you a slice, obviously.

One 9-inch (23 cm) unbaked refrigerated or frozen deep-dish piecrust

6 large eggs

½ cup (120 ml) whole milk

¼ cup (60 ml) heavy cream

½ teaspoon (1.65 g) kosher salt

¼ teaspoon (0.75 g) freshly ground black pepper

1 cup (115 g) cooked ground pork breakfast sausage

2 cups (60 g) baby spinach

4 ounces (115 g) sharp cheddar cheese, cut into ½-inch (1 cm) cubes

Preheat the oven to 375°F (190°C, or gas mark 5).

If the piecrust comes in its own baking pan, place it on a work surface. If it's folded, unfold it and transfer to a 9-inch (23 cm) regular or deep-dish pie pan and flute or crimp the edges, as desired.

In a large bowl, whisk together the eggs, milk, heavy cream, salt, and pepper until well blended.

Sprinkle the sausage, spinach, and cheddar cubes evenly into the piecrust. Pour the egg mixture over the top.

Bake for 30 to 35 minutes, or until the center is fully set and the top is golden brown. Remove from the oven and let cool for 5 to 10 minutes before slicing into eight wedges. Serve warm, or cool completely, cover, and refrigerate for up to 3 days.

Reheat at 375°F (190°C) for 15 to 20 minutes before serving.

JESINIA'S MARGIN NOTES

This quiche holds remarkably well in the freezer. I often prepare two—one for immediate enjoyment and one for future contingencies (academic deadlines, sudden guests, uprisings, etc.). Let it cool completely before wrapping tightly in plastic wrap and sealing in a freezer-safe bag. Keeps for up to 3 months. For best results, thaw overnight in the fridge before reheating.

YIELDS 8 SERVINGS
(½ CUP, OR 81 G)

IMOGEN'S PRE-MORNING RUN GRANOLA

She's up before dawn, braiding her pink hair and tossing handfuls of something that'll stick with her into her mouth. This granola? Just like her: tart first, then unexpectedly sweet. Freeze-dried berries mirror her signature color and attitude, and toasted oats, almonds, and a hint of spice bring enough energy to carry a marked one through morning runs, questionable decisions, or an impromptu sparring match. Best eaten straight from the bag or sprinkled over yogurt.

1¾ cups (230 g) roughly chopped raw almonds

1½ cups (120 g) rolled oats

¼ cup (57 g) packed light brown sugar

½ teaspoon (1.3 g) ground cinnamon

¼ teaspoon (0.8 g) kosher salt

¼ cup (60 ml) melted coconut oil

¼ cup (80 g) maple syrup

¾ cup (64 g) unsweetened desiccated coconut

One 1.2-ounce (34 g) bag unsweetened freeze-dried raspberries or strawberries

Preheat the oven to 350°F (180°C, or gas mark 4). Line a baking sheet with parchment paper.

In a large bowl, stir together the almonds, oats, brown sugar, cinnamon, and salt.

In a small saucepan over low heat, whisk together the coconut oil and maple syrup and heat for 2 to 3 minutes, or until combined fully. Immediately pour the warm mixture over the dry ingredients and stir until coated evenly. Spread into an even layer on the prepared baking sheet.

Bake for 13 minutes. Remove from the oven, sprinkle the coconut over the granola, toss together, and return to the oven. Bake for 3 minutes more, or until golden brown. Watch closely to prevent burning. Let cool completely on the baking sheet.

Once cool, stir in the freeze-dried raspberries.

Store in a sealed bag or airtight container at room temperature for 2 to 3 weeks or freeze for up to 3 months.

YIELDS
1 SERVING

ASHER'S SPICED OVERNIGHT OATS

Before Violet ever trained to fly or wield lightning, she learned to love stories curled beside her father, Asher, in the Scribes' Archives. He wasn't a soldier but a seeker. A seeker of knowledge, of beauty, of meaning written in the margins. These overnight oats are something he might have prepped for himself before a long day among the stacks. It's the kind of breakfast meant to be savored slowly, preferably with a good book and the sound of pages turning.

- ½ cup (40 g) rolled oats
- ½ cup (120 ml) milk of choice
- ¼ cup (60 g) plain whole-milk Greek yogurt
- 1 tablespoon (12 g) chia seeds
- 1 tablespoon (20 g) honey, plus more for topping (optional)
- ¼ teaspoon (1.25 ml) pure vanilla extract
- ¼ teaspoon (0.6 g) ground cinnamon, plus more for topping (optional)
- ¼ teaspoon (0.5 g) ground cardamom
- Grated zest of ½ orange
- Sprinkle of kosher salt
- 1 tablespoon (8.5 g) chopped pistachios and/or walnuts, plus more for topping (optional)

In a pint-size (475 ml) jar or airtight container, combine the oats, milk, Greek yogurt, chia seeds, honey, vanilla, cinnamon, cardamom, orange zest, and salt. Stir until mixed thoroughly. Fold in the pistachios, if using. Seal and refrigerate overnight, or for at least 4 hours.

In the morning, stir again and top with a drizzle of honey, additional nuts, and a sprinkle of cinnamon, if desired.

YIELDS
6 SERVINGS

NAVARRE-FORGED STONE FRUIT AND BERRY MEDLEY

Before the Parapet. Before the sparring mats. Before the Gauntlet bruises, lightning lessons, and aerial combat—there's breakfast. While most cadets grab bread or eggs first, a chilled bowl of fruit is often the only thing that goes down easy before a day of nerve-frying chaos. This medley upgrades the mess hall standard with juicy blackberries, sliced stone fruit, and a bright, herb-laced drizzle of lemon, honey, and extra-virgin olive oil. It's layered but light, sweet with a bite, and, most importantly, one of the few things Violet can trust not to be poisoned. (Probably.) Serve alongside the Wingleader's Wake-Up Quiche (page 16) for a breakfast that'll actually last.

FRUIT MEDLEY

5 ripe nectarines, pitted and sliced

5 ripe plums, pitted and sliced

1 cup (145 g) fresh blackberries

1 cup (155 g) fresh cherries, pitted and halved

8 fresh mint leaves, torn or finely chopped

DRESSING

¼ cup (80 g) honey

2 tablespoons (30 ml) freshly squeezed lemon juice

1 tablespoon (15 ml) extra-virgin olive oil

To make the fruit medley: In a large bowl, combine the nectarines, plums, blackberries, cherries, and mint.

To make the dressing: In a small saucepan over medium heat, whisk together the honey, lemon juice, and olive oil until combined fully and warmed through, 3 to 5 minutes. The mixture should be smooth and pourable. Pour the warm dressing over the fruit and gently toss to coat.

Serve immediately at room temperature or chilled. This dish can be stored in an airtight container in the fridge for up to 3 days.

YIELDS
8 SCONES

ORANGE ZEST SCONES OF RETRIBUTION

Jack Barlowe tried to best Violet more times than we can count, but it was breakfast that took him down first. While we don't recommend poisoning your enemies with pastries, we do recommend serving these warm from the oven, drenched in citrus glaze, and paired with the smug satisfaction of a well-earned win. Crisp at the edges, fluffy in the center, and loaded with orange zest and white chocolate chips, these scones are sweet, sharp, and guaranteed to leave a mark.

Cooking spray, for the baking sheet (optional)

SCONES

- 2 cups (240 g) all-purpose flour, plus more for dusting
- ½ cup (100 g) granulated sugar
- 1 teaspoon (4.6 g) baking powder
- ½ teaspoon (2.3 g) baking soda
- ½ teaspoon (1.65 g) kosher salt
- 1 tablespoon (6 g) grated orange zest
- ½ cup (113 g) cold unsalted butter, cut into small cubes
- ¼ cup (60 g) sour cream
- 1 tablespoon (15 ml) whole milk, plus more as needed
- 1 large egg
- ¾ cup (135 g) white chocolate chips

ORANGE GLAZE

- 1 cup (112 g) powdered sugar
- 2 tablespoons (30 ml) freshly squeezed orange juice
- 1 tablespoon (15 ml) milk of choice
- 1 teaspoon (2 g) grated orange zest
- ¼ teaspoon (1.25 ml) clear vanilla extract

Preheat the oven to 400°F (200°C, or gas mark 6). Line a baking sheet with parchment paper or lightly grease it with cooking spray.

To make the scones: In a large bowl, whisk together the flour, granulated sugar, baking powder, baking soda, salt, and orange zest. Add the butter and cut it into the dry ingredients with a pastry cutter or your fingers until the mixture resembles coarse crumbs.

In a small bowl, whisk together the sour cream, milk, and egg until smooth. Pour the wet ingredients into the flour mixture and stir with a wooden spoon until a shaggy dough forms. Use your hands to gently knead the dough in the bowl until it just comes together. If needed, add more milk, 1 tablespoon (15 ml) at a time—the dough should remain on the drier side. Knead in the white chocolate chips.

Lightly dust a work surface with flour and turn the dough onto it. Pat the dough into an 8-inch (20 cm) round about 1 inch (2.5 cm) thick. Cut into eight wedges (like a pizza) and arrange the wedges evenly spaced on the prepared baking sheet.

Bake for 15 to 18 minutes, or until golden brown and the scones spring back when lightly pressed in the center. They should rise to about 3 inches (7.5 cm) tall. Let cool for 10 minutes before glazing.

To make the orange glaze: In a small bowl, whisk together the powdered sugar, orange juice, milk, orange zest, and vanilla until smooth.

Drizzle over the warm scones and let set for 5 minutes before serving.

JESINIA'S MARGIN NOTES

Work the butter into the flour until the mixture resembles coarse crumbs—think damp sand speckled with pebble-size bits. Those visible flecks of butter? Not a flaw. As they melt, they release steam, creating the lift and tenderness that make these scones a knockout.

YIELDS 12 PASTRY SQUARES

WALWYN PEEL ICED PASTRY SQUARES

Timing is everything, especially when you're baking . . . or sabotaging a rival. Inspired by Violet's ill-fated attempt to dose a pastry with walwyn peel before a challenge match, this flaky, herb-laced square is topped with a punchy grapefruit glaze to get that bitter fruit flavor. The filling is cream cheese based, hiding its sharpness behind a smooth exterior, much like Violet herself. No actual poisons here, of course. Just don't serve them to anyone you like right before combat.

CREAM CHEESE FILLING

8 ounces (225 g) cream cheese, at room temperature

⅓ cup (37 g) powdered sugar

1 teaspoon (5 ml) pure vanilla extract

1 teaspoon (0.8 g) finely chopped fresh thyme leaves

½ cup (120 ml) heavy cream

PASTRY

All-purpose flour, for dusting

Two 17.3-ounce (490 g) packages (4 sheets total) frozen puff pastry, thawed

2 large eggs

1 tablespoon (15 ml) water

GRAPEFRUIT GLAZE

1 cup (112 g) powdered sugar, plus more as needed

2 tablespoons (30 ml) freshly squeezed grapefruit juice, plus more as needed

1 teaspoon (2 g) grated grapefruit zest

Preheat the oven to 400°F (200°C, or gas mark 6). Line two baking sheets with parchment paper.

To make the cream cheese filling: In the bowl of a stand mixer fitted with the paddle attachment, or in a medium bowl using a hand mixer, beat the cream cheese on medium speed until smooth, about 1 minute. Add the powdered sugar, vanilla, and thyme and beat until well mixed.

With the mixer on low speed, slowly pour in the heavy cream. Increase the speed to medium high and whip until the mixture is thick, fluffy, and holds soft peaks, 1 to 2 minutes. Set aside.

To make the pastry: Lightly dust a work surface with flour and unfold the puff pastry sheets on it. Cut each sheet into six 3-by-5-inch (7.5 by 13 cm) rectangles to make twenty-four pieces total.

In a small bowl, beat the eggs and water with a fork to make an egg wash.

Arrange twelve of the pastry rectangles on the prepared baking sheets. Spoon about 2 tablespoons (30 g) of the cream cheese filling into the center of each rectangle, spreading gently to leave a ½-inch (1 cm) border.

Brush the rectangle edges with egg wash. Top with the remaining pastry rectangles and press the edges to seal. Crimp the edges with a fork and prick the tops to vent steam. Brush the tops with more egg wash.

Bake for 15 to 18 minutes, or until puffed and golden brown. Let cool on the baking sheets on wire racks for 10 minutes. They'll be quite puffy.

To make the grapefruit glaze: In a medium bowl, whisk the powdered sugar, grapefruit juice, and grapefruit zest until smooth. Adjust the consistency with extra juice to thin or sugar to thicken.

Drizzle the glaze over the warm squares and let set for 5 minutes before serving. Serve immediately. Store leftover pastries in an airtight container at room temperature for up to 3 days.

YIELDS
12 SANDWICHES

MUSTER AND MARCH SHEET PAN EGG SANDWICHES

These sandwiches were made for mornings when the sun hasn't even breached the peaks and someone's already barking orders. Layered with herby pesto, melty mozzarella, salty ham, and soft-baked eggs, they're assembled en masse on a sheet pan. No one has time for single-serving nonsense before drills. Grab one on your way to the flight field, shove another in a squadmate's hands, and hope you don't burn out before breakfast hits your stomach.

EGGS

- Nonstick cooking spray, for the baking sheet
- 18 large eggs
- ½ cup (120 ml) whole milk
- 1 teaspoon (3.3 g) kosher salt
- ½ teaspoon (1.5 g) freshly cracked black pepper

QUICK PESTO

- 2 cups (60 g) fresh basil leaves
- ½ cup (72 g) toasted pine nuts
- 2 tablespoons (30 ml) freshly squeezed lemon juice
- 1 garlic clove, minced
- ¼ teaspoon (0.8 g) kosher salt
- ¼ teaspoon (0.75 g) freshly cracked black pepper
- ¼ cup (60 ml) extra-virgin olive oil, plus more as needed
- ¼ cup (25 g) grated Parmesan cheese

Preheat the oven to 350°F (180°C, or gas mark 4). Spray an 18-by-13-inch (46 by 33 cm) rimmed baking sheet with cooking spray, line it with parchment paper, and spray the parchment.

To make the eggs: In a large bowl, whisk together the eggs, milk, salt, and pepper until smooth. Pour the eggs onto the prepared baking sheet. Bake for 15 to 18 minutes, or until the eggs are fully set. Let cool completely, then cut into twelve equal rectangles.

To make the quick pesto: In a food processor fitted with the blade attachment, combine the basil, pine nuts, lemon juice, garlic, salt, and pepper. Pulse until finely chopped. With the machine running, drizzle in the olive oil. Add the Parmesan and pulse to incorporate. If needed, add more oil to reach your desired consistency.

SANDWICHES

12 English muffins, split

¼ cup (56 g) salted butter, at room temperature

12 slices Black Forest ham

12 slices mozzarella cheese

Preheat the broiler to 550°F (290°C).

To make the sandwiches: Place the English muffins, cut-side up, on a baking sheet. Spread the butter on each half. Broil for 30 to 60 seconds, or until lightly golden, watching carefully to avoid burning.

Spread about 1 teaspoon (15 g) of the pesto on each of the toasted muffin halves. Leftover pesto can be stored in an airtight container in the fridge for up to a week. On twelve halves, layer 1 egg rectangle, 1 slice of ham, and 1 slice of mozzarella. Top with the remaining muffin halves and serve.

To store, wrap each sandwich tightly in parchment paper or aluminum foil. Place in a freezer-safe zipper-top bag and freeze for up to 2 months (thaw in the refrigerator before reheating) or refrigerate for up to 4 days.

To reheat, remove the parchment or foil:

- Air fryer (recommended): Bake for 5 to 8 minutes at 400°F (200°C).
- Microwave: Remove the foil and heat on high for 90 seconds.
- Oven: Bake at 350°F (180°C, or gas mark 4) for 10 to 12 minutes.

JESINIA'S MARGIN NOTES

After extensive experimentation (including one regrettably soggy attempt), I've found that 30 seconds in the microwave followed by 3 to 5 minutes in an air fryer yields optimal results: a thoroughly heated center and an exterior with just the right crisp. Efficiency and texture. Very satisfying.

YIELDS
2 LOAVES

REBELLION RELIC
BRAIDED BREAD

Marked by the rebellion and twisted by fate, this intricately braided loaf represents the relics that snake up the arms of many of our favorite characters. A swirl of cinnamon, a whisper of espresso, and dark chocolate woven through soft, enriched dough—it tells a story tells a story with every slice. Best served warm, pulled apart with the people you'd burn the world down for.

DOUGH

1 cup (240 ml) warm whole milk, about 100°F (38°C)

One ¼-ounce (7 g) packet active dry yeast (2¼ teaspoons)

4 cups (480 g) all-purpose flour, plus more as needed

½ teaspoon (1.65 g) kosher salt

½ cup (100 g) granulated sugar

1 large egg, at room temperature

1 large egg yolk, at room temperature

⅔ cup (150 g) unsalted butter, cut into 1-inch (2.5 cm) pieces, at room temperature, plus more for the pans

FILLING

1 pound (450 g) dark chocolate, very finely chopped

⅔ cup (133 g) granulated sugar

2 tablespoons (16 g) ground cinnamon

1 tablespoon (6 g) espresso powder

½ cup (113 g) unsalted butter, at room temperature

To make the dough: In the bowl of a stand mixer fitted with the dough hook, or in a large bowl using a hand mixer, combine the warm milk and yeast. Let sit until foamy, about 5 minutes.

In another large bowl, whisk together the flour and salt. Set aside.

Add the sugar, egg, and egg yolk to the yeast mixture and mix on low speed until just combined. With the mixer running, gradually add the flour mixture and mix until incorporated, about 1 minute.

With the mixer on medium speed, add the butter a few pieces at a time. If using a hand mixer, once the dough becomes too stiff to beat, turn it onto a lightly floured surface. Knead by hand until smooth and slightly tacky, about 5 to 10 minutes. If the dough remains too sticky, sprinkle in 1 tablespoon of flour at a time, kneading for 2 to 3 minutes more. Return the dough to the bowl, cover, and let rise in a warm place until doubled in size, about 1 hour.

To make the filling: While the dough rises, in a large bowl, combine the chocolate, sugar, cinnamon, and espresso powder. Add the butter and mash with a fork until combined fully. Set aside.

Continues on page 30

EGG WASH

1 large egg

1 tablespoon (15 ml) water

To make the egg wash: In a small bowl, whisk together the egg and water.

Grease two 9-by-5-inch (23 by 13 cm) loaf pans with butter and set aside.

To finish the dough and make the loaves: Lightly dust a work surface with flour. Punch down the dough and turn it onto the floured surface. Let rest for 5 minutes, then divide the dough in half. Keep one half covered while working with the other half.

Roll one half of the dough into a 14-inch (35 cm) square. Reserve ¼ cup (about 50 g) of the filling, then spread half of the remaining filling evenly over the dough, leaving a ½-inch (1 cm) border. Brush the border with egg wash. Starting from one edge, roll the dough tightly into a log and pinch the seam and ends to seal.

Twist the log lengthwise five or six times. Brush the top with egg wash and gently press half of the reserved filling onto the surface. Bend the log into a horseshoe shape and braid it by crossing one end over the other in a simple two-strand twist. Pinch the ends to seal, twist two more times, and place in a prepared loaf pan.

Repeat with the remaining dough and filling.

Brush the tops of both loaves with egg wash. Cover loosely with a clean kitchen towel and let rise in a warm spot until slightly puffed, about 30 minutes.

Meanwhile, preheat the oven to 350°F (180°C, or gas mark 4).

Bake the loaves, rotating the pans back to front after 30 minutes, for 1 hour, or until lightly golden. Cover with aluminum foil, reduce the oven temperature to 325°F (170°C, or gas mark 3), and bake for another 25 to 30 minutes, or until deep golden brown and an instant-read thermometer inserted into the center reaches 190°F (88°C). (If you don't have a thermometer, the loaf should sound hollow when tapped on the bottom.) Transfer the pans to wire racks and let cool completely in the pans.

To store, let the loaves cool completely, then wrap tightly in plastic wrap. They will keep at room temperature for up to 4 days or in the freezer for up to 3 months.

YIELDS
12 ROLLS

MORNING FORMATION

BREAKFAST "ROLL" CALL

Soft, golden spirals stuffed with scrambled eggs, crispy bacon, and sharp cheddar—these are the breakfast rolls that make you wish morning formation would hold for just five more minutes. Rich and savory with a smoky-sweet glaze, they're the kind of tactical fuel a rider might swipe on the way to the flight field or hoard two of, just in case someone tries to spar before lunch.

DOUGH

½ cup (120 ml) warm water, about 100°F (38°C)

One ¼-ounce (7 g) packet active dry yeast (2¼ teaspoons)

1 teaspoon (4 g) granulated sugar

½ cup (120 ml) whole milk

⅓ cup (75 g) unsalted butter

1 large egg

1 teaspoon (3.3 g) kosher salt

3¾ cups (450 g) all-purpose flour, plus more for dusting

Nonstick cooking spray, for greasing

EGG FILLING

6 large eggs

¼ cup (60 ml) whole milk

½ teaspoon (1.65 g) kosher salt

¼ teaspoon (0.75 g) freshly cracked black pepper

2 teaspoons (9.3 g) unsalted butter, plus 2 tablespoons (28 g) unsalted butter, melted

6 slices bacon, cooked and crumbled

2½ cups (280 g) shredded sharp cheddar cheese, divided

To make the dough: In the bowl of a stand mixer fitted with the dough hook, or in a large bowl using a hand mixer, combine the warm water, yeast, and sugar. Let sit until foamy, about 5 minutes.

In a small saucepan over medium-low heat, warm the milk and butter until the butter melts and the mixture is just warm to the touch. Pour the milk mixture into the yeast mixture, add the egg and salt, and mix until combined. Add the flour, 1 cup (120 g) at a time, mixing on low speed or with a wooden spoon between additions until a soft, slightly tacky dough forms. Knead the dough by hand for 8 minutes, or in a stand mixer with a dough hook for 5 minutes, until smooth and elastic.

Lightly grease a large mixing bowl with cooking spray. Transfer the dough to the prepared bowl, cover with plastic wrap or a clean kitchen towel, and let rise in a warm place until doubled in size, about 45 minutes.

To make the egg filling: In the meantime, in a medium bowl, whisk together the eggs, milk, salt, and pepper. Heat a medium nonstick skillet over medium-low heat. Add 2 teaspoons (9.3 g) of the butter to melt, then pour in the egg mixture. Cook, stirring constantly with a rubber spatula, until soft curds form, about 8 minutes. Remove from the heat and let cool.

Lightly grease a 9-by-13-inch (23 by 33 cm) glass baking dish with cooking spray.

Lightly dust a work surface with flour. Punch down the risen dough and transfer it to the floured surface. Roll the dough into an 18-by-9-inch (46 by 23 cm) rectangle. Evenly spread the scrambled eggs over the dough, followed by the crumbled bacon and 1½ cups (168 g) of the cheddar, leaving a 1-inch (2.5 cm) border along the edges.

Continues on page 33

CHIPOTLE CREAM CHEESE GLAZE

8 ounces (225 g) cream cheese, at room temperature

½ cup (120 g) mayonnaise

1 chipotle pepper (from canned chipotles in adobo)

1 tablespoon (15ml) canned adobo sauce

1 teaspoon (6.7 g) maple syrup

½ teaspoon (1.5 g) garlic powder

¼ teaspoon (0.8 g) kosher salt

Everything bagel seasoning, for topping

Starting from a long edge, roll the dough tightly into a log, tucking in any loose filling. Slice into 12 rolls, each about 1½ inches (3.5 cm) thick. Arrange the rolls, cut-side up, in the prepared baking dish. Cover loosely with plastic wrap and let rise again in a warm place until puffed and touching, about 45 minutes.

Preheat the oven to 400°F (200°C, or gas mark 6).

Brush the tops of the rolls with the remaining 2 tablespoons melted butter. Sprinkle the tops of the risen rolls with the remaining 1 cup (112 g) cheddar. Bake for 25 minutes, then cover loosely with aluminum foil and bake for 5 to 10 minutes more, or until golden brown and bubbling. Let cool in the panfor 10 to 15 minutes before glazing.

To make the chipotle cream cheese glaze: While the rolls bake, in a blender or food processor fitted with the blade attachment, combine the cream cheese, mayonnaise, chipotle pepper, adobo sauce, maple syrup, garlic powder, and salt. Blend until smooth. Spread the glaze generously over the warm rolls.

Sprinkle with everything bagel seasoning and serve immediately. Store leftovers in an airtight container in the fridge for 3 to 5 days.

JESINIA'S MARGIN NOTES

To make the rolls ahead of time (a wise move before early drills or inconvenient rebellions), prepare until the rolls are formed in the baking dish, then cover and refrigerate overnight. Allow 45 minutes at room temperature before proceeding—yeast prefers a gentle return to warmth. If you're in an urgent situation (as everyone seems to be around here), premade pizza dough will suffice.

YIELDS 8 BISCUITS & 1½ CUPS JAM (ABOUT 480 G)

BRENNAN'S HONEYED BISCUITS WITH STRAWBERRY JAM

These golden, flaky biscuits are first served to Violet by her very-much-not-dead brother Brennan in Iron Flame. *She's too stunned to process his concern—but not too stunned to clock how annoyingly good they are. Buttery and tender, brushed with a honey glaze, and best served warm with a quick strawberry jam, they're comforting in the way only food made by someone who knows you can be. Just don't expect her to say thank you right away.*

On that strawberry jam: Later in Iron Flame, *just before practice torture begins in RSC (because sure, that's a normal sentence), Professor Grady offers the cadets biscuits and jam. This is that jam. Sweet, simple, and unassuming—at least until everything goes to hell.*

QUICK STRAWBERRY JAM

- 1 pound (450 g) fresh strawberries, hulled and chopped
- ¾ cup (150 g) granulated sugar
- 2 tablespoons (30 ml) freshly squeezed lemon juice

BISCUITS

- ½ cup (113 g) cold salted butter
- 2 cups (240 g) all-purpose flour, plus more for dusting
- 1 tablespoon (14 g) baking powder
- ½ teaspoon (1.65 g) kosher salt
- ½ cup (120 ml) cold whole milk
- ¼ cup (80 g) honey

To make the quick strawberry jam: In a heavy-bottomed saucepan over medium-low heat, combine the strawberries, sugar, and lemon juice. Cook, stirring frequently, until the sugar dissolves. Increase the heat to medium high and bring the mixture to a boil. Mash the berries slightly and continue to cook, stirring often, until thickened, 10 to 15 minutes. Remove from the heat and let cool in the pot for 10 minutes. Transfer to a pint-size (475 ml) jar and cool to room temperature. Seal and refrigerate until ready to use, or for up to 1 week.

Preheat the oven to 450°F (230°C, or gas mark 8). Line a baking sheet with parchment paper.

To make the biscuits: Using a box grater, grate the butter into a small bowl and freeze until ready to use.

In a large bowl, whisk together the flour, baking powder, and salt. Add the frozen butter and stir to combine.

In a small bowl, whisk together the milk and honey until mostly combined, then pour the honeyed milk into the flour mixture. Stir until a shaggy dough forms.

HONEY BUTTER

2 tablespoons (28 g) salted butter, melted

1 tablespoon (20 g) honey

Lightly dust a work surface with flour and place the dough on it. Knead the dough gently just until no dry bits remain, working quickly to keep the butter cold. Pat the dough into a round 1 inch (2.5 cm) thick. Using a 3-inch (7.5 cm) round biscuit cutter or the rim of a pint glass, cut out biscuits, gathering and reshaping the dough as needed to yield 8 biscuits. Arrange the biscuits on the prepared baking sheet. Bake for 10 to 13 minutes, or until risen and golden.

To make the honey butter: While the biscuits bake, in a small bowl, stir together the melted butter and honey. Brush the tops of the hot biscuits with the honey butter immediately after baking. Serve warm with the strawberry jam.

JESINIA'S MARGIN NOTES

Though it may seem excessive, grating and freezing the butter is the most efficient method I've found for achieving distinct, flaky layers. Cold butter produces steam as it melts, and that steam creates lift—essential for a proper biscuit. Skip this step and you're likely to end up with something closer to a scone. (Not unwelcome, but not the assignment.)

YIELDS
24 MUFFINS

(RIPE) FONILEE BERRY MUFFINS

There's a fine line between fuel and fatal, as every rider knows. This is a great base muffin recipe: reliable, adaptable, and worth keeping in your rotation. The blueberries, our stand-in for fonilee berries, fold into a delicious batter infused with citrus zest and rich olive oil, but blackberries, raspberries, or chopped peaches work just as well. Moist, fragrant, and packed with just enough mystery, they're the kind of breakfast that keeps you alert . . . just in case your squadmate's feeling ambitious.

- 3½ cups (420 g) all-purpose flour
- 2 teaspoons (9.2 g) baking powder
- ½ teaspoon (1.65 g) kosher salt
- 2 cups (400 g) granulated sugar
- 8 large eggs
- 1 tablespoon (6 g) grated orange zest
- 1 tablespoon (6 g) grated lemon zest
- ¾ cup (180 ml) whole milk
- ¾ cup (180 ml) extra-virgin olive oil
- 1½ cups (225 g) fresh blueberries, or (232 g) frozen
- ⅔ cup (66 g) sliced almonds, toasted
- Powdered sugar, for dusting

Preheat the oven to 350°F (180°C, or gas mark 4). Line two 12-cup muffin pans with paper liners.

In a large bowl, whisk together the flour, baking powder, and salt. Set aside.

In the bowl of a stand mixer fitted with the paddle attachment, or in a large bowl using a hand mixer, combine the granulated sugar, eggs, orange zest, and lemon zest and beat on medium-high speed until pale and fluffy, about 3 minutes. Add the milk and mix until incorporated. With the mixer on medium-low speed, slowly stream in the olive oil until fully blended.

Add the flour mixture and mix on low speed until just combined. Gently fold in the blueberries with a spatula, being careful not to overmix. Divide the batter evenly among the prepared muffin cups, filling each nearly to the top. Sprinkle the tops with the toasted almonds.

Bake for 20 to 22 minutes, or until golden brown and a knife inserted into the center comes out with moist crumbs attached. Serve warm or at room temperature. Dust with powdered sugar just before serving.

Leftover muffins can be stored in an airtight container at room temperature for up to 3 days.

Fonilee grows on a vine that looks, to the untrained eye, like common ivy with berries. When ripe, the berries are purple and barely worth eating. Tart enough to make you regret it, but harmless.

The window for doing harm is earlier. Unripe, the berries run a gorgeous lavender, making them easy to spot if you know what you're looking for, especially where the vine tips go white. Pick them, then leave them to dry and grind them finely. The resulting powder is near-white, almost odorless, and completely undetectable in food.

Effects: *Imbalance, severe nausea, difficulty concentrating. Not fatal.*

Location Note: *These berries can be found off the Iakabos River, below the citadel.*

Timing: *Late summer, coming into season. Do not wait for full ripeness.*

JESINIA'S MARGIN NOTES

This is not a recipe. This is a weapons manual. I am annotating it under protest.

The Uaineloidsig line (Greens) didn't build their reputation on instinct. They built it on knowing more than everyone else in the room. Feed the mind accordingly.

2

STUDY SNACKS FIT FOR A SCRIBE

Riders prefer meals that leave grease on the page. Scribes prefer ones that don't. But hunger, unlike Quadrant affiliation, is universal. Eat what keeps your hands steady and your mind sharp.

—Colonel Daxton's Guide to Excelling in the Scribe Quadrant

Scribes reach for focus. Riders reach for fuel. And sometimes, when the world is ending (or the Battle Brief drags into its third hour), they both reach for snacks.

This chapter is for the moments between the mayhem: the hours in the Archives, the strategy sessions that run long, the late-night stakeouts, and the desperate attempts to stay awake through Battle Brief. These are the bites you reach for when you're running on fumes but still need to look sharp (or at least alive). Some are meant to be hoarded, like Nutty Deigh Bites (page 43), and others are best shared across a moment with fellow cadets. "Don't Die" Nachos (page 52), anyone? Just keep something in your pocket that isn't a weapon. You'll thank yourself later.

YIELDS
16 BARS

RECALL BARS

When you're sprinting across the flight field, dodging wyvern, or enduring another punishing session in the weight room, you need fuel that's loyal and dependable, just like your squadmates. Enter Recall Bars: hearty, long-lasting, high-protein snack bars that you can, quite literally, call back to yourself when the need strikes. (Okay, maybe not magically—unless you're Rhiannon Matthias. But it'll feel like magic when you find one tucked into your gear at exactly the right moment.)

- Nonstick cooking spray, for the pan
- 1 cup (226 g) unsalted butter, at room temperature
- 1 cup (225 g) packed light brown sugar
- ½ cup (100 g) granulated sugar
- 2 large eggs
- 2 teaspoons (10 ml) pure vanilla extract
- 1 cup (260 g) creamy peanut butter
- 2½ cups (200 g) rolled oats
- 1 cup (120 g) all-purpose flour
- 1 cup (96 g) chocolate protein powder
- 1 teaspoon (4.6 g) baking soda
- 1 teaspoon (4.6 g) baking powder
- ½ teaspoon (1.65 g) kosher salt
- ¾ cup (135 g) mini unsweetened chocolate chips
- ½ cup (73 g) roasted peanuts, coarsely chopped

Preheat the oven to 350°F (180°C, or gas mark 4). Lightly grease a 9-by-13-inch (23 by 33 cm) baking pan with cooking spray.

In a large bowl, using a hand mixer, beat together the butter, brown sugar, and granulated sugar on medium speed until smooth and light, about 2 minutes.

One at a time, add the eggs and mix well after each addition. Add the vanilla and peanut butter and beat on low speed until combined.

In another large bowl, whisk together the oats, flour, protein powder, baking soda, baking powder, and salt. With the mixer on low speed, gradually add the dry ingredients to the wet ingredients and mix until just combined. Stir in the chocolate chips and peanuts. Press the mixture evenly into the prepared pan.

Bake for 30 to 35 minutes, or until golden brown at the edges and no longer doughy in the center. Let cool completely in the pan on a wire rack before cutting.

Store in an airtight container at room temperature for up to 1 week. Alternatively, wrap each bar in plastic wrap, place in a freezer-safe zipper-top bag, and freeze for up to 6 months.

JESINIA'S MARGIN NOTES

If protein powder isn't available or you prefer to skip it, substitute ½ cup (60 g) all-purpose flour and ½ cup (40 g) unsweetened cocoa powder. The result is slightly less fortified but still sturdy enough to sustain a cadet through drills, research rotations, or minor skirmishes.

YIELDS
18 CLUSTERS

NUTTY DEIGH BITES

Cinnamon laced, citrusy, and just a little sweet, these crunchy nut-and-seed clusters feel like something Liam Mairi might have packed to share with Violet for a long day in the Archives. A little rugged and built to last—just like him—every bite is a reminder. Every bite is a reminder of the kind of kindness that never needed to shout, "It's been my honor."

- Nonstick cooking spray, for the pan
- 1 cup (145 g) raw unsalted almonds
- ½ cup (50 g) raw unsalted pecan halves
- ½ cup (50 g) raw unsalted walnuts
- ½ cup (75 g) raw hulled sunflower seeds
- ½ cup (68 g) raw pumpkin seeds
- ½ cup (43 g) unsweetened coconut flakes
- ⅓ cup (107 g) maple syrup
- 1 large egg white
- 2 teaspoons (10 ml) pure vanilla extract
- ½ teaspoon (1.3 g) ground cinnamon
- ½ teaspoon (1.65 g) kosher salt
- Grated zest of 1 orange

Preheat the oven to 350°F (180°C, or gas mark 4). Line a baking sheet with parchment paper and coat lightly with nonstick cooking spray.

In a large bowl, combine the almonds, pecans, walnuts, sunflower seeds, pumpkin seeds, and coconut flakes.

In a medium bowl, whisk together the maple syrup, egg white, vanilla, cinnamon, salt, and orange zest until frothy. Pour the wet mixture over the nut mixture and stir to coat well. Scoop the mixture into clusters about 2 inches (5 cm) wide and 1 inch (2.5 cm) high on the prepared baking sheet. Use a spoon and your fingers to compress and shape each cluster so it holds together. It will be loose.

Bake for 12 to 16 minutes, or until golden and fragrant. Let cool completely on the baking sheet, about 20 minutes. Store in an airtight container or zipper-top bag at room temperature for up to 1 week.

JESINIA'S MARGIN NOTES

Feel free to substitute your preferred combination of nuts, seeds, or dried fruits. Personalization is encouraged, so long as the overall ratios remain constant. Structure ensures cohesion; within it, there's ample room for creativity. (Much like battle plans . . . or library shelving systems.)

YIELDS
20 BALLS

POPCORN CONDUITS

Conduits are the palm-size glass orbs that help some riders channel and control their signets. Use them too much, and they'll crack under the pressure. These popcorn spheres follow the same philosophy: deceptively simple, absolutely packed with power (read: caramel, sea salt, crushed pretzels, and gooey marshmallow), and likely to disappear faster than you intended. Making the caramel takes a bit of time, but it's a slow burn in the best way. Stick with it, and you'll get something dangerously addictive.

- 1 tablespoon (15 ml) vegetable or canola oil
- ⅓ cup (64 g) popcorn kernels
- 2 cups (100 g) mini marshmallows
- 2 cups (120 g) crushed pretzels
- 1 cup (225 g) packed light brown sugar
- ½ cup (176 g) light corn syrup
- ¼ cup (56 g) unsalted butter
- ⅔ cup (204 g) sweetened condensed milk
- ½ teaspoon (2.5 ml) pure vanilla extract
- ½ teaspoon (2.5 g) flaky sea salt
- Nonstick cooking spray or unsalted butter, for your hands

Pour the oil into a 4-quart (3.8 L) saucepan and set it over high heat. Add the popcorn kernels and cover the pan. Cook, shaking the pan continuously, until the popping slows to a few seconds between pops, 3 to 5 minutes total. Immediately remove from the heat and transfer the popcorn to a large bowl, discarding any unpopped kernels. (Alternatively, use an air popper for this step.)

Add the mini marshmallows and crushed pretzels to the bowl and toss to combine.

In a medium saucepan over medium heat, combine the brown sugar, corn syrup, butter, and sweetened condensed milk. Bring to a gentle boil, stirring frequently. Cook until the mixture reaches 240°F (115°C) on a candy thermometer (soft ball stage), then remove from the heat.

Stir in the vanilla and sea salt. Immediately pour the hot caramel over the popcorn mixture. Stir with a silicone spatula or wooden spoon until coated evenly. Let cool until safe to handle.

Line a baking sheet with parchment paper. Lightly grease your hands with cooking spray. Working quickly, shape the popcorn mixture into palm-size balls (you should get about twenty) and place on the prepared baking sheet. Let cool completely at room temperature.

Store in an airtight container at room temperature for up to 3 days.

YIELDS
20 BITES

CHEESY BUOY BALL BITES

The second ascent of the Gauntlet tests a cadet's balance and nerve: Crossing the infamous buoy line suspended high above the courtyard isn't for the faint of heart. These bites channel that same tension: golden domes of crisp pastry hiding gooey mozzarella cores, brushed with garlic butter and dusted in Parmesan. Served with a punchy dipping sauce, they're rich, buoyant, and slightly dangerous—because once you eat one, you'll be fighting yourself not to eat six.

Nonstick cooking spray, for the baking dish

GARLIC SALT

1 teaspoon (3.3 g) kosher salt

½ teaspoon (1.5 g) garlic powder

½ teaspoon (0.6 g) Italian seasoning

CHEESE BALLS

All-purpose flour, for dusting

One 12.4-ounce (351.5 g) tube refrigerated pizza dough

8 ounces (225 g) ciliegine-size fresh mozzarella cheese balls, about 20 balls

2 tablespoons (28 g) salted butter, melted

1¾ teaspoons garlic salt (add between butter and Parmesan cheese)

¼ cup (25 g) grated Parmesan cheese

DIPPING SAUCE

1 cup (245 g) tomato sauce

¼ cup (65 g) tomato paste

½ teaspoon (1.65 g) kosher salt, plus more as needed

½ teaspoon (0.6 g) Italian seasoning, plus more as needed

½ teaspoon (1.5 g) garlic powder, plus more as needed

¼ teaspoon (0.45 g) cayenne pepper, plus more as needed (optional)

Preheat the oven to 400°F (200°C, or gas mark 6). Lightly grease an 8-by-8-inch (20 by 20 cm) glass baking dish with cooking spray.

To make the garlic salt: In a small bowl, stir together the salt, garlic powder, and Italian seasoning. Set aside.

To make the cheese balls: Lightly dust a work surface with flour. On the floured surface, roll the pizza dough into a rectangle that is 8 by 10 inches (20 by 25 cm) and ⅛ inch (3 mm) thick. Cut into twenty equal squares. Place a mozzarella ball in the center of each square. Gather the dough around the cheese ball and pinch the edges to seal. Arrange the sealed balls, seam-side down, in the prepared baking dish.

Brush the tops of the wrapped cheese balls with melted butter. Sprinkle evenly with the garlic salt and Parmesan.

Bake for 10 to 12 minutes, or until the tops are golden and the cheese is melted.

To make the dipping sauce: While the bites bake, in a small bowl, stir together the tomato sauce, tomato paste, salt, Italian seasoning, garlic powder, and cayenne (if using). Taste and adjust the seasoning if needed.

Let the bites cool for 5 to 10 minutes before transferring to a serving platter. Serve warm with the dipping sauce.

JESINIA'S MARGIN NOTES

If time or supply constraints arise, store-bought marinara will serve. Should mozzarella balls prove elusive, simply cut fresh mozzarella into 1-inch (2.5 cm) cubes.

YIELDS
6 SERVINGS

INFERNO WINGS

Named for the fiery breath of dragons, these grilled wings bring the heat in a way that would make even Tairn nod in approval. Coated in a bold spice rub and finished with a quick char, they're smoky, blistered, and unapologetically hot.

Vegetable or canola oil, for the grill grates, or nonstick cooking spray, for the baking sheets

SPICE RUB

¼ cup (56 g) packed light brown sugar
¼ cup (28 g) sweet paprika
2 teaspoons (5 g) chili powder
1 teaspoon (3 g) garlic powder
1 teaspoon (2.3 g) onion powder
1 teaspoon (3.3 g) kosher salt
½ teaspoon (1.5 g) freshly cracked black pepper
½ teaspoon (0.9 g) cayenne pepper

3 pounds (1.4 kg) party-style chicken wings (drumettes and flats separated)

SMOKY SAUCE

1 cup (225 g) ketchup
½ cup (120 ml) apple cider vinegar
½ cup (113 g) packed light brown sugar
¼ cup (85 g) molasses
3 tablespoons (21 g) smoked paprika
2 teaspoons (5 g) chili powder
2 teaspoons (6 g) garlic powder
2 teaspoons (4.6 g) onion powder
1 teaspoon (5 ml) hot sauce (such as Tabasco)
1 teaspoon (5 ml) Worcestershire sauce
¼ teaspoon (0.45 g) cayenne pepper
¼ teaspoon (0.8 g) kosher salt

Preheat an outdoor grill to medium-high heat and brush the grill grates clean. If using an oven, preheat to 400°F (200°C, or gas mark 6). Line two rimmed baking sheets with aluminum foil and coat with cooking spray.

To make the spice rub: In a small bowl, stir together all the spice rub ingredients.

Pat the wings dry with paper towels and place them in a large bowl. Sprinkle with about half of the spice rub and toss to coat, adding more as needed to cover evenly and ensure a bold flavor. You may not need all of it. Store any leftover rub in an airtight container at room temperature for up to 3 months.

If grilling: Lightly grease the grill grates. Arrange the wings in a single layer on the grill grates over direct heat, making sure they are not touching. Grill for 15 to 20 minutes, flipping every 5 minutes, until the internal temperature reaches 165°F to 175°F (74°C to 79°C) and the wings are lightly charred.

If baking: Arrange the wings in a single layer on the prepared baking sheets. Bake for 15 minutes, flip, then bake for 10 to 15 minutes more, or until the internal temperature reaches 165°F to 175°F (74°C to 79°C) and the wings are golden brown.

To make the smoky sauce: While the wings cook, in a saucepan over medium-high heat, combine all the sauce ingredients. Bring to a simmer, stirring frequently, then simmer for 5 minutes, or until smooth and slightly thickened.

Transfer the cooked wings to a clean large bowl. Pour half of the sauce over the wings and toss to coat. Add more sauce to taste. Refrigerate extra sauce in an airtight container for up to 1 week.

Serve immediately.

JESINIA'S MARGIN NOTES

These are best grilled. Don't shy away from a bit of char; it adds depth. If baking, a brief turn under the broiler (a minute or two) will encourage blistering. Controlled flame, properly applied, is rarely a bad idea.

YIELDS
8 SERVINGS

SORRENGAIL'S SECRETS STUFFED DATES

The Sorrengail name is synonymous with loyalty, ambition . . . and dangerous secrets. These deceptively simple stuffed dates are a nod to those hidden layers: tender and honeyed on the outside but hiding a rich, savory center of goat cheese and spiced nuts. Trust carefully. Bite boldly.

- ⅓ cup (45 g) finely chopped pistachios
- 2 teaspoons (1.2 g) minced fresh rosemary leaves
- 1 teaspoon (2 g) grated orange zest
- 2 teaspoons (10 ml) freshly squeezed orange juice
- ¼ teaspoon (0.6 g) ground cinnamon
- ¼ teaspoon (1.2 g) flaky sea salt
- 1 tablespoon (15 ml) extra-virgin olive oil
- 12 ounces (340 g) pitted Medjool dates
- 8 ounces (225 g) fresh goat cheese, at room temperature
- Hot honey, for garnish (optional)

Preheat the oven to 375°F (190°C, or gas mark 5). Line a rimmed baking sheet with parchment paper.

In a small bowl, stir together the pistachios, rosemary, orange zest, orange juice, cinnamon, sea salt, and olive oil. Mix to coat the nuts well. Set aside.

Using a small, sharp knife, slice each date open lengthwise (do not cut all the way through). Gently open each date and fill with 1 to 2 teaspoons (5 to 10 g) of the goat cheese. Arrange the stuffed dates, cut-side up, on the prepared baking sheet. Spoon 1 to 2 teaspoons (5 to 10 g) of the pistachio mixture into each date.

Bake for 15 minutes, or until the dates have softened and the filling is fragrant. Remove from the oven and let sit for 5 minutes. Transfer to a serving platter and drizzle with hot honey, if using. Serve warm.

YIELDS 16
DEVILED EGGS

"VENINED"
EGGS WITH FRIED SHALLOTS

With crimson veins lacing pale whites and a center that packs a sharp bite, these deviled eggs are for the venin. The red marbled exterior mimics their telltale eyes, while the filling delivers an unapologetic punch of horseradish, echoing the pain they project into their victims. Unlike the wielders, though, we're providing some relief with a crown of crispy fried shallots. Just don't underestimate them. Plan accordingly: the longer the soak, the deeper the red eyes.

EGGS

- 8 large eggs
- Red food coloring, for the dye bath
- ¼ cup (60 g) mayonnaise
- 1 tablespoon (15 g) Dijon mustard
- 1 tablespoon (15 g) prepared horseradish (optional)
- 1 tablespoon (4 g) chopped fresh dill
- ½ teaspoon (1.65 g) kosher salt
- ¼ teaspoon (0.75 g) freshly ground black pepper
- ¼ teaspoon (0.75 g) garlic powder

FRIED SHALLOTS

- 2 tablespoons (30 ml) extra-virgin olive oil
- 1 large shallot, thinly sliced (about ¼ cup, or 40 g)
- ¼ teaspoon (0.8 g) kosher salt

To make the eggs: Place the eggs in a large saucepan and fill with enough cold water to cover. Bring to a boil over high heat, then cook for 12 minutes.

While the eggs boil, prepare an ice bath in a large bowl. When the eggs are done, transfer them to the ice bath and let cool for 10 to 15 minutes.

Meanwhile, prepare the dye bath. In a large bowl, stir 5 or 6 drops of red food coloring into 3 inches (7.5 cm) of water. Add more food coloring, as needed, for a deeper red hue.

Remove the eggs from the ice bath and gently crack the shells by rolling them on the counter. The cracks should penetrate the membrane slightly but not peel the shell completely. Submerge the cracked eggs in the dye bath. Add water as needed to cover the eggs fully. If they float, use a ceramic plate to weigh them down. Refrigerate the eggs to soak for at least 3 hours or up to 12 hours. The longer the soak, the more vibrant the marbling.

Peel the soaked eggs and halve them lengthwise. Scoop the yolks into a medium bowl and arrange the whites, cut-side up, on a platter.

Add the mayonnaise, mustard, horseradish (if using), dill, salt, pepper, and garlic powder to the yolks. Mash with a fork until smooth and combined fully. Transfer the filling to a zipper-top bag, snip off one corner, and pipe the filling into the egg whites.

To make the fried shallots: Line a plate with paper towels. In a small skillet over medium-high heat, heat the olive oil. Add the shallot and cook, stirring frequently, until golden brown, 3 to 5 minutes. Transfer to the prepared plate and season with the salt, then let cool for 5 minutes. Top the eggs with the fried shallot slices and serve immediately. Store leftovers in the refrigerator for up to 3 days.

YIELDS
6 TO 8 SERVINGS

"DON'T DIE"
NACHOS

Technically, these nachos offer little nutritional value. Emotionally, however? Lifesaving. Ridoc swears by them as the perfect fuel for surviving Battle Brief, RSC torture drills, or spontaneous venin attacks. He'd say, "I make them for the squad. But mostly for me. You're welcome."

QUICK-PICKLED RED ONIONS

1 medium red onion, very thinly sliced

½ cup (120 ml) water

½ cup (120 ml) distilled white vinegar

2 tablespoons (25 g) granulated sugar

2 tablespoons (20 g) kosher salt

To make the quick-pickled red onions: Pack the onion slices into a pint-size (475 ml) Mason jar or heat-safe container. In a small saucepan over medium heat, combine the water, vinegar, sugar, and salt. Bring to a gentle simmer and cook, stirring frequently, until the sugar dissolves, about 1 minute. Carefully pour the hot liquid over the onion slices. Use a spoon to press the onion into the brine. Let cool to room temperature, 20 to 30 minutes. Cover and refrigerate until ready to use. They are best within 3 days but will keep for 2 to 3 weeks.

As customizable as your signet, these nachos are ideal for eating straight from the tray with your bare hands while huddled around a dwindling campfire.

Want to eat like the whole squad?

- *Rhiannon: Extra sour cream and pickled onions*
- *Sawyer: No spice, add more beans*
- *Violet: Minimal toppings, maximum melted cheese*
- *Ridoc: All of the above, plus a second plate—"for balance"*

Nonstick cooking spray, for the pan

NACHOS

1 pound (450 g) ground beef

One 1¼-ounce (35.4 g) packet taco seasoning

¼ cup (60 ml) water

One 16-ounce (450 g) jar salsa, divided

One 12-ounce (340 g) bag tortilla chips

One 15-ounce (425 g) can black beans, drained and rinsed

1½ cups (170 g) shredded Mexican cheese blend

2 jalapeño peppers, cored, seeded, and thinly sliced (optional)

1 handful fresh cilantro leaves

Sour cream, for serving

Preheat the oven to 400°F (200°C, or gas mark 6). Line a baking sheet with aluminum foil and coat with cooking spray.

To make the nachos: In a large skillet over medium heat, cook the ground beef, breaking it apart with a spatula, until browned, 12 to 15 minutes. Drain the excess fat. Return the skillet to the heat and stir in the taco seasoning and water. Cook, stirring occasionally, until the liquid is absorbed. Stir in ½ cup (130 g) of the salsa and remove from the heat.

Arrange the tortilla chips in a single layer on the prepared baking sheet. Top evenly with the seasoned beef and black beans. Sprinkle with the cheese.

Bake for 5 to 8 minutes, or until the cheese is melted and the nachos are heated through.

Drain the pickled onions and scatter them over the nachos. Top with the jalapeños (if using) and cilantro. Serve warm with sour cream and the remaining salsa on the side.

*Reds run hot and they don't wait.
Approach from the left, keep your
eyes down, and for the gods' sake,
get something in you before
they run out of patience.*

3

MIDDAY FUEL

Cadets are allotted no more than twenty uninterrupted minutes for mid-cycle nourishment unless otherwise excused for injury, interrogation, or death.

—*Article Four, Section Nine,* The Dragon Rider's Codex

Lunch at Basgiath isn't about leisure. Whether you're emerging from flight drills, dodging venin, or finally getting five blessed minutes between classes, you need something that hits hard, fuels fast, and doesn't fall apart in your hands.

This chapter gathers quick meals for riders who are running on grit, adrenaline, and just enough sleep to function. From the comfort of tomato soup to wraps and sandwiches, these recipes are practical without being boring, bold without being fussy. Some, like the Riorson House Chopped Salad(page 63), feel like healing in a bowl.

These aren't banquet meals. These are refueling stations. Make 'em fast, eat 'em faster, and get back to the fight.

YIELDS
6 SERVINGS

BASGIATH MESS HALL TURKEY MELT

A proper sandwich—melty, savory, and stacked high—feels like luxury compared to the standard field rations riders choke down on long patrols. This one's inspired by those rare moments at Basgiath when the mess hall actually delivers: roasted turkey layered with smoky bacon, juicy tomatoes, provolone, and a swipe of pesto aioli, all pressed between slabs of focaccia until crisp and golden. It's simple, satisfying, and just indulgent enough to make you feel human again after a grueling flight rotation.

Want to go the extra mile? Make the Stone Table Bread with Rosemary and Sea Salt (page 105) instead of buying focaccia. It's sturdy, flavorful, and makes these sandwiches feel even more satisfying.

PESTO AIOLI

½ cup (120 g) mayonnaise

2 tablespoons (30 g) prepared pesto

1 teaspoon (5 ml) freshly squeezed lemon juice

SANDWICH

One 12-by-8-inch (30 by 20) loaf focaccia

2 tablespoons (30 ml) extra-virgin olive oil

12 ounces (340 g) sliced roasted turkey

6 slices thick-cut bacon, cooked until crisp

2 medium tomatoes, thinly sliced

6 slices provolone cheese

Preheat the broiler, using the high setting if available, 550°F (290°C).

To make the pesto aioli: In a small bowl, whisk together the mayonnaise, pesto, and lemon juice. Set aside.

To make the sandwich: Halve the focaccia loaf horizontally. Place both halves, cut-side up, on a baking sheet and brush with the olive oil. Broil for 1 to 2 minutes, or until golden and toasted. Watch carefully to avoid burning. Set aside.

Turn the oven temperature to 350°F (180°C, or gas mark 4).

Spread the pesto aioli evenly over the toasted sides of the bread halves. Layer the turkey, bacon, tomato slices, and provolone on the bottom half of the bread, in that order. Place the top half, cut-side down, on top.

Transfer the sandwich to the oven and bake for 7 to 10 minutes, or until the cheese is melted and the top is golden and crisp. Watch closely to prevent overbrowning.

Remove from the oven and let rest for 5 minutes. Slice into six squares and serve warm.

JESINIA'S MARGIN NOTES

If you're headed to strategy drills or a flight rotation, know that this sandwich travels well and tastes just as satisfying cold. Skip the oven altogether. I've packed it for long shifts in the Archives more times than I can count—no reheat required, no flavor lost.

JESINIA'S MARGIN NOTES

Both the mushroom filling and the herbed yogurt spread may be prepared up to 3 days in advance and stored separately in the fridge. A bit of forethought ensures a swift and satisfying assembly later, even amidst chaos.

YIELDS
4 WRAPS

MELTY LEIGHORREL MUSHROOM WRAPS

Leighorrel mushrooms may have tripped up Violet's opponent on the mat, but here they play a far less treacherous role. Inspired by the mind-fogging fungi she once weaponized, these wraps feature caramelized onions, sautéed mushrooms, and sweet roasted peppers tucked into a warm wrap with a creamy, yogurt spread. No hallucinations here, just a plant-forward lunch that hits hard and melts beautifully.

HERBED YOGURT SPREAD

1 cup (240 g) plain whole-milk Greek yogurt
2 tablespoons (8 g) chopped fresh parsley
2 tablespoons (8 g) chopped fresh dill
1 tablespoon (15 ml) freshly squeezed lemon juice
1 garlic clove, finely grated
¼ teaspoon (0.8 g) kosher salt
¼ teaspoon (0.75 g) freshly ground black pepper

WRAP FILLING

2 tablespoons (30 ml), extra-virgin olive oil, divided, plus more for brushing
1 large yellow onion, thinly sliced
8 ounces (225 g) cremini mushrooms, sliced
4 ounces (115 g) oyster mushrooms, torn into bite-size pieces
One 12-ounce (340 g) jar roasted red peppers, drained and sliced
½ teaspoon (1.65 g) kosher salt
¼ teaspoon (0.75 g) freshly ground black pepper
1 teaspoon (5 ml) balsamic vinegar

4 large flour tortillas or lavash wraps
8 slices provolone or mozzarella cheese

To make the herbed yogurt spread: In a small bowl, stir together the yogurt, parsley, dill, lemon juice, garlic, salt, and pepper. Cover and refrigerate until ready to use.

To make the wrap filling: In a large skillet over low heat, heat 1 tablespoon (15 ml) of the olive oil. Add the onion and cook, stirring occasionally, until golden and deeply caramelized, 20 to 25 minutes. If the onion starts to burn, add a splash of water. Push the onion to the edges of the pan and add the remaining 1 tablespoon (15 ml) olive oil.

Add the cremini and oyster mushrooms. Cook for 2 to 3 minutes, without stirring to encourage browning, then stir occasionally until the mushrooms are tender and browned, 6 to 8 minutes total.

Add the roasted red peppers, salt, pepper, and vinegar. Stir to combine and cook for 1 minute until just warmed through. Remove from the heat.

To assemble the wraps: Spread a generous amount of herbed yogurt on each tortilla or lavash wrap. Divide the mushroom mixture evenly among the wraps and top each with two slices of cheese.

Roll up the wraps like a burrito, tucking in the sides, or fold in half like a quesadilla. Brush lightly with olive oil.

Wipe out the skillet and place it over medium heat. Place the wraps in the skillet, working in batches as needed, and toast for 2 to 3 minutes per side, or until the outside is golden and the cheese has melted. Slice and serve warm.

YIELDS
6 SERVINGS

SCRIBE'S PARCHMENT PIE

Light, flaky, and layered, this savory pie is a nod to the meticulous art of recordkeeping that underpins the world of Basgiath's scribes. The crisp, delicate phyllo layers echo the parchment pages of a well-worn codex. Crackling as you cut through them, they reveal a filling of spinach, lemon, feta, and herbs that's as thoughtful and composed as any carefully kept manuscript. It's the kind of midday dish you could also imagine passing around during late-night strategy sessions, fueling minds as sharp as the layers are crisp.

- 3 tablespoons (45 ml) extra-virgin olive oil, plus more for the pan
- 5 cups (7 ounces, or 200 g) fresh spinach, or 5 ounces (140 g) frozen spinach, thawed and drained
- ½ cup (3 ounces, or 85 g) crumbled feta cheese
- ⅓ cup (21 g) finely chopped fresh parsley
- 2 tablespoons (8 g) chopped fresh dill
- 2 tablespoons (12 g) finely sliced green onion
- 2 teaspoons (10 ml) freshly squeezed lemon juice
- 1 teaspoon (2 g) grated lemon zest
- ¼ cup (28 g) finely chopped oil-packed sun-dried tomatoes
- 2 large eggs
- ½ teaspoon (1.65 g) kosher salt
- ¼ teaspoon (0.75 g) freshly cracked black pepper
- 7 sheets phyllo dough, thawed if frozen
- Flaky sea salt

Preheat the oven to 350°F (180°C, or gas mark 4). Lightly brush or spray an 8- or 9-inch (20 or 23 cm) springform pan with olive oil.

If using fresh spinach, place it in a large microwave-safe bowl and sprinkle with 1 tablespoon (15 ml) water. Microwave on high power for 1 to 2 minutes, or until wilted. Let cool slightly, then squeeze out as much moisture as possible using the back of a spoon or clean hands. Roughly chop the spinach and transfer to a large mixing bowl. If using frozen spinach, place the thawed and drained spinach in the bowl.

Add the feta, parsley, dill, green onion, lemon juice, lemon zest, sun-dried tomatoes, eggs, salt, and pepper to the spinach. Stir until combined thoroughly.

Drape 1 sheet of phyllo dough into the prepared pan, letting about half hang over the edge. Lightly brush the exposed surface with olive oil. Repeat with the remaining phyllo sheets, rotating each slightly to cover the bottom and sides of the pan evenly, brushing each layer with olive oil as you go.

Spoon the spinach filling into the center of the pan and gently press to level it. Fold the overhanging phyllo over the filling, scrunching the layers slightly to create texture. Brush the top with the remaining olive oil and sprinkle with sea salt.

Bake for 30 to 35 minutes, or until the phyllo is golden brown and crisp. Let cool for 5 to 10 minutes before slicing. Serve warm or at room temperature.

YIELDS
4 SERVINGS

RIORSON HOUSE CHOPPED SALAD

After the brutal battle at Resson, Violet and her surviving friends find themselves in Aretia—battered, grieving, and in desperate need of healing. If there was ever a moment when food became medicine, it would be this. This hearty chopped salad is exactly the kind of restorative meal the healers at Riorson House might champion: crunchy greens and raw vegetables for bite, creamy avocado and feta for richness, and bright, lemony tahini dressing to wake up the palate. Toss in smoky roasted chickpeas and pepperoni, if you like, for extra substance, and you've got a salad that's grounding, energizing, and just indulgent enough to remind you you're alive.

ROASTED CHICKPEAS

One 15-ounce (425 g) can chickpeas, drained and rinsed

1 tablespoon (15 ml) extra-virgin olive oil

½ teaspoon (1.5 g) garlic powder

½ teaspoon (1.15 g) smoked paprika

½ teaspoon (1.65 g) kosher salt

LEMON-TAHINI DRESSING

1 small shallot, finely chopped (¼ cup, or 40 g)

1 tablespoon (15 ml) freshly squeezed lemon juice

1 tablespoon (15 g) tahini

2 teaspoons (10 ml) red wine vinegar

2 teaspoons (10 g) Dijon mustard

2 tablespoons (30 ml) extra-virgin olive oil

¼ teaspoon (0.25 g) dried oregano

¼ teaspoon (0.75 g) garlic powder

¼ teaspoon (0.8 g) kosher salt

¼ teaspoon (0.75 g) freshly cracked black pepper

Preheat the oven to 425°F (220°C, or gas mark 7). Line a baking sheet with parchment paper.

To make the roasted chickpeas: Dry the chickpeas thoroughly with a clean kitchen towel, removing as many skins as possible. Spread the chickpeas in a single layer on the prepared baking sheet and toss with the olive oil, garlic powder, paprika, and salt. Roast for 20 to 25 minutes, shaking the pan halfway through, until golden and crispy. Let cool on the baking sheet.

To make the lemon-tahini dressing: In a small bowl, whisk together the shallot, lemon juice, tahini, vinegar, mustard, olive oil, oregano, garlic powder, salt, and pepper until emulsified. Alternatively, combine the ingredients in a jar with a lid, cover, and shake well. Set aside.

Continues on page 64

SALAD

1½ cups (72 g) chopped romaine lettuce

1 cup (135 g) diced Persian or English cucumber

1 red bell pepper, diced

1 cup (85 g) finely chopped Brussels sprouts

¾ cup (135 g) quartered cherry tomatoes

⅓ cup (55 g) diced red onion

⅓ cup (40 g) chopped pepperoncini

¼ cup (33.5 g) diced pepperoni or salami (optional)

¼ cup (85 g) crumbled feta cheese

1 ripe avocado, diced

1 tablespoon (4 g) minced fresh dill

Flaky sea salt and freshly cracked black pepper

To make the salad: In a large bowl, combine the romaine, cucumber, bell pepper, Brussels sprouts, tomatoes, red onion, and pepperoncini. Pour half of the dressing over the salad and toss well to combine.

Add the pepperoni (if using), feta, avocado, dill, and the roasted chickpeas. Drizzle with the remaining dressing and season with sea salt and pepper to taste. Toss gently and serve immediately.

YIELDS
4 FLATBREADS

RIDER'S RATION FETA FLATBREAD

Some days at Basgiath, you don't have time for anything elaborate. You just need something hearty, fast, and good enough to keep you on your feet through drills, flights, and sparring matches. This quick flatbread fits the bill: gooey mozzarella, tangy feta, a drizzle of olive oil, and a sprinkle of black caraway, all crisped on soft pita. It's the kind of simple, sturdy meal a rider could throw together between muster and maneuvers, either on the grill or in the air fryer (for us, anyway).

4 pitas

2 cups (230 g) shredded mozzarella cheese, divided

1 cup (170 g) crumbled feta cheese, divided

4 tablespoons (60 ml) extra-virgin olive oil, divided

1 teaspoon (5 g) flaky sea salt, divided

1 teaspoon (2.2 g) black caraway seeds, divided

To grill: Preheat a grill to medium-high heat and brush the grill grates clean.

To air fry: Preheat an air fryer to 380°F (195°C).

To broil: Preheat the broiler, using the high setting if available.

Line up the pita breads. If broiling , put them on a baking sheet. Top each with ½ cup (58 g) of the mozzarella and ¼ cup of the feta (43 g). Drizzle each with 1 tablespoon (15 ml) of the olive oil, then sprinkle with ¼ teaspoon (1.25 g) of the sea salt and ¼ teaspoon (0.55 g) of the black caraway seeds.

Grill over direct heat for 5 to 7 minutes, air fry (one at a time) for 4 to 6 minutes, or broil for 2 to 3 minutes, or until the cheese is melted and the edges of the pita are golden or lightly charred. Slice into triangles and serve immediately.

JESINIA'S MARGIN NOTES

Seeking additional protein? Leftover slices of the Diplomatic Roasted Chicken (page 75) layer beautifully atop this flatbread. Efficient, satisfying, and, like any good accord, better the second day.

YIELDS
6 HAND PIES

BODHI'S
RIGHT-HAND MAN PIES

This isn't flashy food, it's get-shit-done food. The kind of meal tucked into a rider's pack before a recon flight or slipped to a squadmate who's skipped too many meals. Ground lamb is simmered with garlic and onion, then hit with cinnamon, oregano, and just enough red pepper to raise an eyebrow. Melty cheese holds it all together. Baked inside flaky, golden crusts, these hand pies are hearty, portable, and strategic. Exactly the kind of thing Bodhi would make . . . if he cooked. (He doesn't.) Serve with the Daggertail Root Roast (page 99) and you've got yourself a meal.

FILLING

1 tablespoon (15 ml) extra-virgin olive oil

½ large or 1 small yellow onion, diced

2 garlic cloves, minced

8 ounces (225 g) ground lamb or ground beef

½ teaspoon (0.5 g) dried oregano

½ teaspoon (1.65 g) kosher salt

¼ teaspoon (0.6 g) ground cinnamon

¼ teaspoon(0.75 g) freshly ground black pepper

¼ teaspoon (0.3 g) red pepper flakes (optional)

To make the filling: In a large skillet over medium heat, heat the olive oil. Add the onion and cook until softened, stirring occasionally, 3 to 5 minutes. Add the garlic and cook for 1 minute.

Add the lamb and cook, breaking it up with a spatula, until browned and cooked through, 5 to 7 minutes. Drain any excess fat.

Stir in the oregano, salt, cinnamon, black pepper, and red pepper flakes (if using). Remove from the heat and let cool slightly.

Preheat the oven to 400°F (200°C, or gas mark 6). Line two baking sheets with parchment paper.

Continues on page 68

PIES

All-purpose flour, for dusting

One 14-ounce (400 g) package refrigerated piecrusts (2 crusts), at room temperature

¾ cup (84 g) shredded Italian cheese blend (fontina, mozzarella, provolone, or similar), divided

1 large egg

1 tablespoon (15 ml) water

Flaky sea salt

DIPPING SAUCE

1 cup (240 g) mayonnaise

4 garlic cloves, minced

3 tablespoons (27 g) capers

2 teaspoons (10 g) Dijon mustard

2 teaspoons (10 ml) freshly squeezed lemon juice

½ teaspoon (1.65 g) kosher salt

¼ teaspoon (0.75 g) freshly cracked black pepper

To make the pies: Lightly dust a work surface with flour and unroll the piecrusts on it. Use a 5-inch (13 cm) round cutter (or trace a small bowl with a paring knife) to cut out six rounds, gathering and rerolling scraps as needed.

Sprinkle each round with about 1½ tablespoons (14 g) of the cheese. Spoon 2 to 3 tablespoons (40 to 60 g) of the lamb filling on top of the cheese, leaving a ½-inch (1 cm) border around the edge. Fold the dough over to create a half-moon shape. Use a fork to crimp the edges and seal. Transfer the hand pies to the prepared baking sheets 1 inch (2.5 cm) apart.

In a small bowl, whisk the egg and water. Brush the tops of the hand pies with the egg wash and sprinkle with sea salt. Cut two or three small slits in the top of each pie to vent steam.

Bake for 13 to 15 minutes, or until golden brown. Let cool slightly before serving.

To make the dipping sauce: While the pies bake, in a medium bowl, stir together the mayonnaise, garlic, capers, mustard, lemon juice, salt, and black pepper until well combined.

Serve the hand pies warm with the dipping sauce on the side.

YIELDS
6 SERVINGS

LILITH'S CHARRED TOMATO AND ROASTED GARLIC SOUP

If there's any meal that feels like it could weather a storm (or spark one), it's this. Inspired by General Sorrengail herself, this soup blends the boldness of fire with the comfort of home. Charring the tomatoes adds smoky depth in honor of Lilith's storm-wielding signet, while roasted garlic brings its own quiet intensity. It's the kind of meal you'd imagine Violet being served in a rare warm moment with her mother—not the general.

1 head garlic

3 tablespoons (45 ml) extra-virgin olive oil, divided

2½ pounds (1.1 kg) ripe Roma tomatoes, halved

1 medium yellow onion, cut into large chunks

2 teaspoons (6.6 g) kosher salt, divided

One 14-ounce (400 g) can tomato sauce

½ cup (120 ml) chicken or vegetable broth

1 teaspoon (4 g) granulated sugar

½ teaspoon (1.5 g) freshly ground black pepper

¼ teaspoon (0.3 g) red pepper flakes

¼ teaspoon (0.45 g) cayenne pepper

½ cup (120 ml) heavy cream

2 tablespoons (5 g) chopped fresh basil, plus 2 tablespoons (5 g) julienned fresh basil

4 ounces (115 g) Asiago cheese, shaved

Preheat the oven to 450°F (230°C, or gas mark 8). Line two baking sheets with aluminum foil.

Cut out a 6-inch (15 cm) square of foil. Slice the top off the head of garlic to expose the cloves. Place the garlic in the center of the foil, drizzle with 1 tablespoon (15 ml) of the olive oil, and wrap the foil around the garlic to form a sealed packet. Place the wrapped garlic on one of the prepared baking sheets.

Divide the tomatoes and onion between the two prepared baking sheets and drizzle with the remaining 2 tablespoons (30 ml) olive oil. Sprinkle with 1 teaspoon (3.3 g) of the salt.

Roast for 30 to 35 minutes, or until the tomatoes are collapsed and everything is fragrant. Let cool slightly.

Set aside the wrapped garlic. Transfer the roasted tomatoes and onion to a large stockpot. Add the tomato sauce, broth, remaining 1 teaspoon (3.3 g) salt, sugar, black pepper, red pepper flakes, and cayenne. Bring to a simmer over medium-high heat and cook for 10 minutes, stirring occasionally. Remove from the heat.

Squeeze the roasted garlic cloves from the bulb and stir them into the soup. Add the cream and chopped basil. Use an immersion blender to purée the soup until smooth. If using a standard blender, work in batches and let the soup cool slightly before blending.

Ladle the soup into bowls and garnish with the Asiago and julienned basil. Serve warm.

The most powerful line does not celebrate lightly. When a black calls the feast, you sit down, you eat everything, and you don't ask questions.

4

FEASTS AFTER FLIGHT

Among the great traditions of the Riders Quadrant is the evening meal shared after a successful campaign. There, united by victory and tempered by loss, dragon and rider alike may return to what is most essential: order, nourishment, and peace.

—Navarre, an Unedited History *by Colonel Lewis Markham*

Once the swords are sheathed, the dragons fed, and the squad's mended, there's one more thing to face: hunger. This chapter is built for the evenings when victories outnumber bruises. These are the meals that feel earned—feasts that bring warmth back into your bones whether you're curled up near the fire at Aretia, crowding into the Basgiath mess hall, or eating in silence next to your fiercest allies.

You'll find bold roasts, restorative stews, battle-won sliders, and food that doesn't bite back. Meals for after the fight, or before the next one. Because, even in Navarre, peace never lasts long.

YIELDS
4 SERVINGS

VIOLENT LITTLE KEBABS

"You really are a violent little thing, aren't you?" Xaden teased. If Violet had served him these skewers, he might have meant it even more. Marinated sirloin and flame-kissed vegetables bring heat and attitude in equal measure, making these quick-to-vanish kebabs the perfect fare for a post-sparring feast. Best devoured outside with your squad, preferably with ash still in your hair and a grin on your face. These are even better served alongside Flame-Kissed Corn on the Cob (page 101).

MARINADE

¼ cup (60 ml) soy sauce

1 tablespoon (15 ml) extra-virgin olive oil

1 tablespoon (15 ml) freshly squeezed lemon juice (from ½ lemon)

1 tablespoon (15 ml) Worcestershire sauce

1 tablespoon (15 g) Dijon mustard

1 tablespoon (14 g) packed light brown sugar

1 tablespoon (9 g) garlic powder

1 tablespoon (3.6 g) Italian seasoning

½ teaspoon (0.6 g) red pepper flakes

¼ teaspoon (0.75 g) freshly ground black pepper

KEBABS

1½ pounds (680 g) top sirloin steak, cut into 1-inch (2.5 cm) cubes

1 red bell pepper, cut into 1-inch (2.5 cm) pieces

1 yellow bell pepper, cut into 1-inch (2.5 cm) pieces

8 ounces (225 g) button mushrooms

1 red onion, cut into 1-inch (2.5 cm) pieces

To make the marinade: In a medium bowl, whisk together all the marinade ingredients.

To make the kebabs: Pour half of the marinade into a large zipper-top bag or lidded container, add the steak, and seal the bag. Pour half of the remaining marinade into a second large zipper-top bag or lidded container, add the bell peppers, mushrooms, and onion, and seal the bag. Pour the remaining marinade into a small jar or bowl for serving. Shake the bags, or stir, to coat the meat and vegetables evenly. Refrigerate for at least 1 hour or up to overnight.

When ready to cook, thread the marinated steak and vegetables onto eight metal skewers, alternating pieces and leaving space between them for even cooking. Brush the assembled kebabs with any leftover marinade from the vegetable container. Discard any remaining marinade used for raw ingredients.

Preheat a grill to medium-high heat. Brush the grill grates clean.

Place the kebabs on the grill grates over direct heat and grill for 6 to 10 minutes, turning every couple of minutes, until the steak reaches your preferred doneness and the vegetables are lightly charred.

Transfer to a platter and let rest for 5 minutes. Serve warm with the reserved marinade as a dipping sauce.

DIPLOMATIC
ROASTED CHICKEN

Tensions may run high in the halls of Basgiath, but they're higher still at feasts with tentative allies and potential traitors. Regardless, a roasted chicken always shows up, no matter who's seated at the table. This version is rubbed with smoky paprika and garlic butter for golden skin, while lemon and fresh oregano perfume the meat from within. Whether you're breaking bread with a sworn enemy, stalling during negotiations, or trying to eat before the next ambush, this meal proves that sometimes the only common ground is what's on the table. Serve with Vidirys Cauliflower Stuffing (page 100) to make sure your stomach is full for long back and forths.

- One 5- to 6-pound (2.3 to 2.7 kg) whole roasting chicken
- Kosher salt and freshly ground black pepper
- 1 large bunch fresh oregano, plus 10 sprigs
- 1 lemon, halved
- 1 head garlic, halved horizontally
- 1 teaspoon (3 g) garlic powder
- 1 tablespoon (7 g) sweet paprika
- ¼ cup (56 g) unsalted butter, at room temperature
- 1 large yellow onion, thickly sliced
- 4 carrots, cut into 2-inch (5 cm) chunks
- 1 bulb fennel, fronds removed, cut into wedges
- Extra-virgin olive oil, for drizzling

Adjust an oven rack to the lower-middle position and preheat the oven to 425°F (220°C, or gas mark 7).

Remove the giblets from the chicken. Trim away any excess fat or pin feathers and pat the chicken dry inside and out with paper towels.

Generously season the inside of the cavity with salt and pepper. Stuff the cavity with the bunch of oregano, both lemon halves, and the halved garlic head.

In a small bowl, stir together the garlic powder, paprika, and butter. Gently lift the skin over the breast and thighs and spread some of the butter mixture directly onto the meat without tearing the skin. Rub the remaining butter mixture all over the surface of the chicken. Season the outside with more salt and pepper. Tie the legs together with kitchen twine and tuck the wing tips under the body.

In a large roasting pan or on a rimmed baking sheet, combine the onion, carrots, and fennel. Drizzle with olive oil, season with salt and pepper, and scatter the oregano sprigs over the top. Toss to coat and spread into an even layer. Place the chicken on top of the vegetables.

Roast for about 1½ hours, or until the juices run clear when you cut between the leg and thigh and an instant-read thermometer inserted into the thickest part of the thigh reads 165°F (74°C).

Transfer the chicken and vegetables to a serving platter and tent loosely with aluminum foil. Let rest for 20 minutes before carving.

Serve warm with the vegetables spooned alongside.

YIELDS
6 SERVINGS

RIDER'S RECOVERY SMOKY CHICKPEA AND CHORIZO STEW

After a brutal day, even the toughest rider needs a meal that restores body and spirit. This smoky, spicy stew of chorizo, chickpeas, potatoes, and fire-roasted tomatoes is just the thing to get you back on your feet. Bold, hearty, and layered with warmth, it's exactly what you'd want simmering in a mess-hall kitchen after surviving another day at Basgiath. Top it with a cooling lemon-garlic yogurt sauce to balance the heat—and don't forget the Stone Table Bread with Rosemary and Sea Salt (page 105) on the side for dunking.

STEW

1 pound (450 g) loose Mexican pork chorizo

1 small yellow onion, diced

3 garlic cloves, minced

1 tablespoon (7 g) smoked paprika

1 teaspoon (1 g) dried oregano

½ teaspoon (1.65 g) kosher salt

¼ teaspoon (0.75 g) freshly cracked black pepper

1 dried bay leaf

One 14-ounce (400 g) fire-roasted tomatoes

One 14-ounce (400 g) chickpeas, drained and rinsed

2 pounds (900 g) red potatoes, cut into ½-inch (1 cm) cubes

4 cups (950 ml) chicken broth

3 cups (90 g) baby spinach

LEMON-GARLIC YOGURT SAUCE

1 cup (240 g) plain full-fat Greek yogurt

1 tablespoon (15 ml) freshly squeezed lemon juice

1 small garlic clove, minced or grated

¼ teaspoon (0.8 g) kosher salt

To make the stew: In a stockpot over medium heat, cook the chorizo, breaking it apart with a spatula, until fully browned, 12 to 15 minutes. Transfer the cooked chorizo to a bowl and drain the fat into a heat-safe container. Once cooled, discard the fat (do not pour it down the drain).

Return the chorizo to the pot and add the onion and garlic. Sauté over medium heat until fragrant, 1 to 2 minutes. Stir in the smoked paprika, oregano, salt, and pepper. Cook for 1 minute.

Add the bay leaf, tomatoes and their juices, chickpeas, potatoes, and chicken broth. Stir to combine and bring to a simmer. Reduce the heat to medium low and cook, stirring occasionally, for 15 to 20 minutes, or until the potatoes are fork-tender.

To make the lemon-garlic yogurt sauce: While the stew simmers, in a small bowl, stir together the yogurt, lemon juice, garlic, and salt until smooth. Set aside.

Remove and discard the bay leaf. Stir in the spinach and cook for 1 to 2 minutes, until just wilted.

Ladle the stew into bowls and top with a generous dollop of the yogurt sauce. Serve hot.

JESINIA'S MARGIN NOTES

If the stew proves a touch too fiery for your liking (or for the company you're keeping), substitute loose mild Italian sausage for the chorizo. The result is still hearty and flavorful, just . . . less likely to provoke tears. Culinary ones, at least.

YIELDS
4 SERVINGS

VARRISH'S "WEAK POINT" GLAZED RIBS

Every opponent has a weakness, even if you have to break a few bones (or ribs) to find it. These slow-cooked pork ribs are inspired by Burton Varrish's ruthless talent for exploiting vulnerabilities . . . though, unlike him, this dish wins you over with tender meat and smoky sauce, not cruelty. Coated in a punchy dry rub and seared for bite, the ribs melt into a molasses-laced glaze spiked with vinegar, paprika, and just enough cayenne to keep your defenses up. Pair with Flame-Kissed Corn on the Cob (page 101) to soften the blow.

One 2-pound (900 g) rack pork spare ribs

RIBS

2 tablespoons (28 g) packed light brown sugar

1 teaspoon (3.3 g) kosher salt

1 teaspoon (3 g) garlic powder

1 teaspoon (2.3 g) onion powder

½ teaspoon (1.5 g) freshly cracked black pepper

Smoky Sauce (see Inferno Wings, page 47)

Preheat the oven to 400°F (200°C, or gas mark 6). Line a large baking sheet with aluminum foil. Alternatively, preheat a grill to medium-high heat and brush the grill grates clean.

To prep the ribs: Pat the spare ribs dry and flip them bone-side up. Slide your fingers under the corner of the thin membrane and peel it off with a paper towel for grip. Trim any thick pieces of fat.

In a small bowl, stir together the brown sugar, salt, garlic powder, onion powder, and black pepper. Rub the mixture generously over both sides of the ribs. Place the ribs on the prepared baking sheet.

Roast for 15 minutes, then flip and roast for 10 minutes more until the ribs are browned. Alternatively, grill over direct heat for about 10 minutes per side.

To make the smoky sauce: While the ribs cook, make the sauce as directed.

Transfer the ribs to a large slow cooker, meat-side facing outward along the inner wall. If needed, cut the rack into sections to fit. Pour half of the sauce over the ribs, coating thoroughly. Reserve the remaining sauce for serving.

Cover and cook on low heat for 4 to 6 hours, or until the meat is very tender but still clings to the bone.

Serve warm, slathered with the reserved sauce.

YIELDS
8 SERVINGS

TYRRENDOR HEARTH CHICKEN STEW

Hearty, simple, and rich with flavor, this stew tastes like something that could've been simmering in a cast-iron pot over one of Tyrrendor's stone hearths long before war reshaped the kingdom. Chicken thighs are seared and then braised in a garlicky tomato broth, while red potatoes and sliced carrots soak up every drop. Briny green olives and sweet peas cut through the richness for balance. It's the kind of meal that fortifies for battle, whether you're riding out to defend the wards or just surviving another brutal day at Basgiath. Serve with Stone Table Bread with Rosemary and Sea Salt (page 105) to soak up every last drop of broth.

- 6 bone-in, skin-on chicken thighs
- 1½ teaspoons kosher salt and ½ teaspoon freshly ground black pepper, plus more for seasoning
- 2 tablespoons (30 ml) extra-virgin olive oil
- ½ yellow onion, diced
- ½ cup (75 g) sliced carrots
- 2 tablespoons (20 g) chopped garlic
- 4 cups (950 ml) chicken broth
- One 28-ounce (800 g) can diced tomatoes
- 2 tablespoons (32 g) tomato paste
- 1½ pounds (680 g) red potatoes, cut into 1-inch (2.5 cm) cubes
- 3 dried bay leaves
- ¼ teaspoon (0.3 g) red pepper flakes (optional)
- 1 cup (130 g) frozen peas
- ½ cup (77.5 g) green olives (such as Castelvetrano)
- ½ cup (32 g) chopped fresh parsley

Season the chicken thighs on both sides with salt and pepper.

In a large Dutch oven or heavy-bottomed pot over medium-high heat, heat the olive oil. Working in batches if needed, place the chicken thighs, skin-side down, in the pot and sear until deeply golden, 4 to 5 minutes per side. Transfer to a plate.

Reduce the heat to medium. Add the onion and carrots to the pot and cook, stirring occasionally, until softened, 5 to 7 minutes. Stir in the garlic and cook until fragrant, about 1 minute.

Return the chicken to the pot. Add 1½ teaspoons salt (5 g), ½ teaspoon (1.5 g) pepper, the chicken broth, diced tomatoes and their juices, tomato paste, potatoes, bay leaves, and red pepper flakes (if using). Stir to combine.

Increase the heat to high and bring to a boil. Reduce the heat to medium and simmer, uncovered, for 15 to 20 minutes, or until the potatoes and carrots are fork-tender and the interior of the chicken has reached 165°F (74°C) when tested with an instant-read thermometer.

Remove and discard the bay leaves. Transfer the chicken to a cutting board and let cool slightly. Stir the peas and olives into the stew and remove from the heat.

Once cool enough to handle, remove the chicken meat and discard the skin and bones, then shred or tear the meat into bite-size pieces. Return the chicken to the pot and stir to combine. Bring the soup back to a gentle simmer before serving.

Garnish with the parsley and serve warm.

YIELDS
6 SERVINGS

TAIRN'S FEAST SHEPHERD'S PIE

This one's for the dragon from the ancient line, our favorite fire-breathing curmudgeon we'd trust with our lives. If dragons threw a victory feast, this dish would be at the center of the table . . . likely served after they'd helped themselves to the shepherd's flock. Ground beef is simmered with ale, rosemary, and deeply caramelized onions, creating a base that's as bold and layered as Tairn's battle strategy. On top, a golden crown of mashed potatoes laced with smoked Gouda, because this dragon would never settle for bland. It's old-school comfort, the kind of meal that demands silence, respect, and maybe a second helping.

MEAT FILLING

2 tablespoons (30 ml) extra-virgin olive oil

1 large yellow onion, thinly sliced

1 pound (450 g) lean ground beef (90/10)

2 teaspoons (1.2 g) chopped fresh rosemary leaves

1 teaspoon (3.3 g) kosher salt

½ teaspoon (1.5 g) freshly ground black pepper

2 tablespoons (30 ml) Worcestershire sauce

2 garlic cloves, minced

2 tablespoons (15 g) all-purpose flour

¼ cup (64 g) tomato paste

½ cup (120 ml) beef broth

½ cup (120 ml) dark beer (such as Guinness)

1 cup (160 g) frozen peas and carrots

Nonstick cooking spray, for the baking dish

To make the meat filling: In a large skillet over medium heat, heat the olive oil. Reduce the heat to low, add the onion, and cook, stirring occasionally, until deeply caramelized, 25 to 30 minutes. (Tip: This is a good time to start your potato topping.)

Increase the heat to medium and add the ground beef. Break up the meat with a spatula and stir in the rosemary, salt, and pepper. Cook for 6 to 8 minutes, or until browned.

Stir in the Worcestershire sauce and garlic and cook for 1 minute. Add the flour and tomato paste and stir until fully incorporated, with no streaks remaining. Pour in the broth and beer and add the peas and carrots. Increase the heat to medium high and bring the mixture to a simmer. Reduce the heat to medium low and simmer for 5 minutes, stirring occasionally, until the mixture thickens slightly. Remove from the heat and cover.

Preheat the oven to 400°F (200°C, or gas mark 6). Grease a 9-by-9-inch (23 by 23 cm) baking dish or 9-inch (23 cm) deep-dish pie pan with cooking spray.

POTATO TOPPING

1 pound (450 g) russet potatoes (about 1 large), peeled and cut into 1-inch (2.5 cm) cubes

1 pound (450 g) yellow potatoes (about 4 small), peeled and cut into 1-inch (2.5 cm) cubes

¼ cup (56 g) salted butter

¼ cup (60 ml) half-and-half

½ teaspoon (1.5 g) garlic powder

1 teaspoon (3.3 g) kosher salt

¼ teaspoon (0.75 g) freshly ground black pepper

8 ounces (225 g) smoked Gouda cheese, shredded

To make the potato topping: Place the potatoes in a large pot and cover with cold water. Bring to a boil over high heat, then reduce the heat to medium and cook the potatoes until fork-tender, 10 to 12 minutes. Drain the potatoes and return them to the hot pot. Add the butter, half-and-half, garlic powder, salt, and pepper. Mash until smooth. Stir in the Gouda until melted and incorporated fully.

Transfer the meat mixture to the prepared baking dish and spread into an even layer. Spoon the mashed potatoes over the top and spread gently to cover.

If your baking dish is very full, place it on a rimmed baking sheet to catch any overflow. Bake for 25 to 30 minutes, or until the edges are bubbling and the top begins to turn golden. Let cool for 15 minutes before serving.

JESINIA'S MARGIN NOTES

To make this truly worthy of an ancient, fire-breathing dragon, substitute lamb or goat for the ground beef, if you can procure it. Both offer a richer, more robust flavor befitting a dish that might be served in the aftermath of battle, when even dragons pause to savor the spoils.

YIELDS
6 SERVINGS

"WE DO NOT EAT OUR ALLIES" VEGETARIAN CHILI

"We do not eat our allies," Tairn's infamous declaration, echoed through the flight field and, thankfully, reached the kitchens. This chili makes sure there's no need to eye your squad with suspicion: It's so hearty, even a feathertail would think twice before taking a bite out of a friend. Beans simmer in a smoky tomato base layered with warm spices, cocoa, cinnamon, and a hit of adobo heat. It's the perfect meal for squad gatherings, late-night strategy sessions, or anytime you need to fuel up without committing any betrayals.

2 tablespoons (30 ml) extra-virgin olive oil

1 red and 1 green bell pepper, finely chopped

1 yellow onion, finely chopped

4 garlic cloves, minced

2 tablespoons (32 g) tomato paste

1 chipotle pepper in adobo, minced, plus 1 teaspoon (5 ml) adobo sauce (optional)

1 teaspoon (5 ml) canned adobo sauce (optional)

1 tablespoon (5 g) unsweetened cocoa powder

1 tablespoon (7.5 g) chili powder

2 teaspoons (2 g) dried oregano

1 teaspoon (2.3 g) ground cumin

½ teaspoon (1.3 g) ground cinnamon

One 28-ounce (800 g) can fire-roasted diced tomatoes

2 cups (475 ml) vegetable broth

One 15.5-ounce (440 g) can pinto beans, drained and rinsed

One 15.5-ounce (440 g) can black beans, drained and rinsed

1 teaspoon (3.3 g) kosher salt

½ teaspoon (1.5 g) freshly cracked black pepper

Chopped fresh cilantro, sour cream, tortillas chips, avocado slices, and/or radish slices, for garnish

In a large stockpot or Dutch oven over medium-high heat, heat the olive oil. Add the red and green bell peppers and onion. Cook, stirring occasionally, for about 10 minutes, or until softened.

Add the garlic, tomato paste, chipotle chile (if using), adobo sauce (if using), cocoa powder, chili powder, oregano, cumin, and cinnamon. Stir to coat the vegetables and cook for 2 minutes, until fragrant and the spices are toasted.

Stir in the diced tomatoes and their juices, vegetable broth, pinto beans, and black beans. Season with the salt and pepper. Bring to a gentle simmer. Reduce the heat to medium low, partially cover the pot, and simmer for 25 to 30 minutes, stirring every 10 minutes, until slightly thickened and the flavors have melded. Taste and adjust the seasoning if needed.

Ladle into bowls and top with any combination of chopped fresh cilantro, sour cream, avocado slices, thinly sliced radishes, and tortilla chips.

YIELDS
12 SLIDERS

SCORCHED
HERD SLIDERS

If anyone's in the business of taking down a herd of sheep, it's Andarna—even if she prefers goats. After all, she's the dragon who once declared, "We should seek sheep," with the same gravity others reserve for battle plans. These charred, juicy lamb sliders are for her: small but fierce, a little chaotic, and completely unbothered by authority. Spiced with harissa and topped with creamy feta and bright pickled onions, they're quick to vanish, just like our favorite feathertail when something fluffy crosses the horizon. Serve hot with Flame-Kissed Corn on the Cob (page 101), and don't hesitate to swap in beef, if you prefer.

PICKLED RED ONIONS

1 medium red onion, very thinly sliced

½ cup (120 ml) water

½ cup (120 ml) distilled white vinegar

2 tablespoons (25 g) granulated sugar

2 tablespoons (20 g) kosher salt

LAMB PATTIES

4 garlic cloves, minced

1 tablespoon (4 g) chopped fresh parsley

1 tablespoon (1 g) chopped fresh cilantro

1 tablespoon (1.5 g) chopped fresh mint

2 pounds (900 g) ground lamb

2 tablespoons (30 g) harissa

2 teaspoons (6.6 g) kosher salt

To make the pickled red onions: Pack the red onion into a pint-size (475 ml) Mason jar or heat-safe container. In a small saucepan, combine the water, vinegar, sugar, and salt. Bring to a simmer over medium heat, stirring until the sugar and salt dissolve. Pour the hot liquid over the onion and let cool. Seal the jar and refrigerate until ready to use.

To make the lamb patties: In a large bowl, combine the garlic, parsley, cilantro, mint, lamb, harissa, and salt. Using your hands or a rubber spatula, mix thoroughly until combined evenly. Form the lamb mixture into twelve patties, about 3 inches (7.5 cm) wide and 2½ ounces (75 g) each. Refrigerate for at least 30 minutes.

HARISSA MAYO

½ cup (120 g) mayonnaise

Juice of ½ lemon

1 tablespoon (15 g) harissa

FOR ASSEMBLY

4 tablespoons (60 ml) extra-virgin olive oil, divided

12 slider buns or dinner rolls (such as potato or brioche), split

⅔ cup (115 g) crumbled feta cheese

To make the harissa mayo: In a small bowl, whisk together the mayonnaise, lemon juice, and harissa until smooth. Refrigerate until ready to serve.

To cook and assemble: Preheat a grill to medium-high heat and brush the grill grates clean. Alternatively, cook the patties on the stovetop.

If cooking on the stovetop, in a large skillet over medium-high heat, heat 2 tablespoons (30 ml) of the olive oil until shimmering. Add the patties in batches and cook for 8 to 10 minutes total, flipping halfway through, until browned and cooked to your liking. Transfer to a plate and repeat with the remaining patties.

If grilling, grill the patties over direct heat for 3 to 5 minutes per side, or until well browned and cooked to your liking.

If cooking on the stovetop, preheat the oven to 450°F (230°C, or gas mark 8) before you begin cooking the patties. Then, as the patties cook, arrange the buns, cut side up, on a baking sheet. Brush with the remaining 2 tablespoons (30 ml) olive oil. Bake for 3 to 4 minutes, or until golden brown, watching carefully. If grilling, brush the cut side of the buns with oil as directed, then place the cut side down on the grill and toast for 1 to 2 minutes.

Spread the harissa mayo on both halves of the buns. On each bottom half, layer some crumbled feta and a few pickled onion slices. Place a lamb patty on top and finish with the top bun.

Serve immediately while warm.

YIELDS
8 SERVINGS

CAT'S CLAW SPICY CALABRIAN CHILI PASTA WITH SAUSAGE

Cat doesn't just cut you with words, she pulls your feelings to the surface and lights them on fire. This spicy pasta channels that same energy: savory Italian sausage, garlicky tomato sauce, Calabrian chili paste that lingers long after the first bite, and a bit of zesty lemon just to keep you on your toes. It's bold and guaranteed to stir something in you, like rage, longing, adrenaline . . . or all three at once. Just like Cat. Pair this pasta with Stone Table Bread with Rosemary and Sea Salt (page 105) to provide a little relief from the heat.

1 tablespoon (15 ml) extra-virgin olive oil

3 garlic cloves, minced

1 pound (450 g) ground mild Italian sausage

One 24-ounce (680 g) can tomato sauce

2 tablespoons (30 g) chopped Calabrian chilis

½ teaspoon (1.65 g) kosher salt

¾ cup (180 ml) heavy cream

1 pound (450 g) rigatoni, cooked according to the package directions

2 cups (60 g) baby spinach

1 cup (100 g) grated Parmesan cheese, plus more for serving

2 teaspoons (4 g) grated lemon zest

1 tablespoon (15 ml) freshly squeezed lemon juice (from about ½ lemon)

Fresh basil, julienned, for garnish

In a large skillet over medium heat, heat the olive oil. Add the garlic and sauté for 1 to 2 minutes, or until fragrant but not browned. Add the ground sausage and cook, breaking it apart with a spatula, until browned and cooked through, 10 to 12 minutes. Stir in the tomato sauce, Calabrian chilis, and salt. Simmer for 10 minutes, stirring occasionally, until the flavors meld.

Pour in the heavy cream and return the sauce to a gentle simmer. Cook for 2 to 3 minutes, or until the sauce thickens slightly.

Add the cooked rigatoni and toss to coat. Stir in the spinach, Parmesan, lemon zest, and lemon juice. Cook for 1 to 2 minutes, or until the spinach wilts and the cheese melts.

Serve warm, topped with additional Parmesan and fresh basil.

YIELDS
12 ROLL-UPS

ROLLING LOG LASAGNA

The log staircase in the Gauntlet has claimed plenty of cadets, but these rolled lasagnas will leave you feeling nothing but victorious. Sheets of pasta are layered with ricotta and bold meat sauce, then rolled up tighter than a cadet clinging for dear life. Serve them at your Gauntlet Eve Carbo Load, preferably without the threat of shattered bones looming over the meal.

Kosher salt

12 lasagna noodles

Nonstick cooking spray, for the baking dish

MEAT SAUCE

4 cups (1 kg) marinara sauce, divided

1 tablespoon (15 ml) extra-virgin olive oil

1 small or ½ large yellow onion, diced

8 ounces (225 g) ground beef

8 ounces (225 g) ground Italian sausage (hot or mild)

3 garlic cloves, minced

CHEESE FILLING

One 15-ounce (425 g) container ricotta cheese

1 large egg

3 cups (345 g) shredded mozzarella cheese, divided

½ cup (50 g) grated Parmesan cheese

1 tablespoon (3.6 g) Italian seasoning

½ teaspoon (1.65 g) kosher salt

¼ teaspoon (0.75 g) freshly ground black pepper

In a large pot of boiling salted water, cook the noodles until al dente. Drain and lay flat on parchment paper to cool.

While the noodles cook, preheat the oven to 375°F (190°C, or gas mark 5). Lightly grease a 9-by-13-inch (23 by 33 cm) baking pan with cooking spray.

To make the meat sauce: Spread ½ cup (132 g) of the marinara sauce over the bottom of the prepared dish and set the dish aside. In a large skillet over medium heat, heat the olive oil, add the onion, and cook, stirring occasionally, for about 10 minutes, or until softened. Add the beef and sausage and cook, breaking the meat up with a spatula, for 8 to 10 minutes, or until browned. Drain off the excess fat. Stir in the garlic and the remaining marinara sauce and simmer for 10 minutes to meld the flavors. Remove from the heat.

To make the cheese filling: In a medium bowl, stir together the ricotta, egg, 2 cups (230 g) of the mozzarella, the Parmesan, Italian seasoning, salt, and pepper until well mixed.

To make the rolls: Spread about 2 tablespoons (about 30 g) of the cheese mixture evenly across each lasagna noodle. Top each with about ¼ cup (60 g) of the meat sauce, reserving the rest for topping. Roll up each noodle tightly, keeping the filling inside, and place the rolls, seam-side down, in the prepared baking dish. Spoon the remaining meat sauce evenly over the top and sprinkle with the remaining 1 cup (115 g) mozzarella.

Lightly coat one side of a sheet of aluminum foil large enough to cover the dish with cooking spray and place it, sprayed-side down, over the dish. Bake for 35 minutes, or until the cheese is completely melted and the lasagna rolls are warmed through. For a golden, bubbly top, uncover the dish, turn the oven to broil, and broil for 1 to 2 minutes, watching carefully to prevent burning.

Let cool slightly before serving.

YIELDS 4 SERVINGS

DARK WIELDER'S MUSHROOM RISOTTO WITH BLACKBERRY REDUCTION

Theophanie doesn't shout. She doesn't need to. Like a storm gathering on the horizon, her presence darkens the room long before lightning strikes. This risotto is a tribute to that quiet, elemental power. Earthy mushrooms, caramelized until nearly blackened, melt into creamy rice enriched with sharp white cheddar, then finished with a glossy blackberry-thyme reduction that cuts through the richness like a well-placed lie. Best eaten slowly, with one eye on the sky—maybe looking out for a certain blue daggertail? Sgaeyl's Spritz (page 145) pairs perfectly with this dish.

RISOTTO

2 tablespoons (30 ml) extra-virgin olive oil

¾ cup (75 g) thinly sliced shallot (from 1 or 2 shallots)

2 cups (168 g) sliced, stemmed shiitake mushrooms

¼ teaspoon (0.8 g) kosher salt

¼ teaspoon (0.75 g) freshly ground black pepper

1 tablespoon (15 ml) soy sauce

2 teaspoons (1.6 g) chopped fresh thyme leaves, plus 2 tablespoons (4.8 g)

1 cup (200 g) arborio rice

¼ cup (60 ml) dry white wine

4 cups (950 ml) vegetable broth

¾ cup (84 g) shredded sharp white cheddar cheese, plus more for garnish

BLACKBERRY-THYME REDUCTION

1 cup (145 g) fresh blackberries, or (151 g) frozen

2 tablespoons (40 g) honey

1 teaspoon (0.8 g) fresh thyme leaves

1 tablespoon (15 ml) balsamic vinegar

Pinch of kosher salt

To make the risotto: In a large skillet over medium heat, heat the olive oil. Add the shallot and cook, stirring frequently, until softened, 3 to 4 minutes. Add the mushrooms, salt, pepper, and soy sauce. Cook, stirring occasionally, until the mushrooms are deeply browned and caramelized, 10 to 12 minutes. Stir in 2 teaspoons (1.6 g) of the thyme leaves and cook for 1 minute.

Add the rice and cook, stirring constantly, for 1 minute to lightly toast it. Pour in the white wine and cook until mostly absorbed, about 2 minutes.

Begin adding the broth, ½ cup (120 ml) at a time, stirring frequently and letting each addition absorb before adding more. Maintain a gentle simmer throughout. Continue until the rice is creamy and al dente, 25 to 30 minutes total.

To make the blackberry-thyme reduction: While the risotto cooks, in a small saucepan, combine the blackberries, honey, thyme leaves, vinegar, and salt. Bring to a boil over medium heat, then reduce the heat to maintain a simmer. Cook, stirring occasionally, until slightly thickened, 10 to 12 minutes. Strain through a fine-mesh sieve into a heat-safe bowl and set aside.

When the risotto is done, remove it from the heat and stir in the cheddar. Taste and adjust the seasoning if needed.

To serve, divide the risotto among four bowls. Drizzle with the blackberry-thyme reduction and garnish with additional cheddar and the remaining 2 tablespoons (4.8 g) chopped thyme leaves. Serve warm.

JESINIA'S MARGIN NOTES

This dish is an excellent companion to the "Marked by Flame" Grilled Steak with Rosemary Marinade (page 92). The flavors complement one another like well-matched sparring partners: distinct, but stronger together.

YIELDS
4 SERVINGS

"MARKED BY FLAME" GRILLED STEAK WITH ROSEMARY MARINADE

Some meals are earned, not handed to you. This steak doesn't beg for attention; it seizes it, like a rider just bonded, maybe even burned. A bold rosemary-garlic marinade infuses every bite with flavor. Charred over open flame—or seared in a cast-iron skillet if duty calls you indoors—it's the kind of meal that demands to be eaten with your hands, grease on your fingers and grit in your teeth. Just survived Threshing? This is what you eat next, ideally with a side of "Better Than You Think" Broccoli with Feta and Shallots (page 102).

MARINADE

½ cup (120 ml) soy sauce

2 tablespoons (30 ml) extra-virgin olive oil

2 tablespoons (3.4 g) minced fresh rosemary leaves

1 tablespoon (7 g) sweet paprika

1 tablespoon (7.5 g) chili powder

1 tablespoon (9 g) garlic powder

2 teaspoons (2 g) dried oregano

1½ teaspoons (4.5 g) freshly cracked black pepper

STEAKS

Four 8- to 10-ounce (225 to 285 g) sirloin steaks, about 1 inch (2.5 cm) thick

1 tablespoon (14 g) salted butter (if cooking in a skillet)

To make the marinade: In a medium bowl, whisk together the soy sauce, olive oil, rosemary, paprika, chili powder, garlic powder, oregano, and pepper.

To marinate the steaks: Place the steaks in a large zipper-top bag or shallow dish. Pour the marinade over the steaks, turn to coat, then seal or cover. Refrigerate for at least 1 hour or up to 8 hours, turning once or twice.

Remove the steaks from the refrigerator 30 minutes before cooking. Discard the marinade and pat the steaks dry with paper towels.

To cook in a skillet: Heat a large cast-iron skillet over medium-high heat until very hot, about 3 minutes. Add the butter and let it melt. Cook the steaks in batches, if needed, 4 to 7 minutes per side, depending on doneness. Reduce the heat slightly if the pan begins to smoke excessively.

Transfer the steaks to a plate and tent loosely with aluminum foil. Let rest for 5 to 10 minutes before serving.

To grill: Preheat a grill to medium-high heat and brush the grill grates clean. Lightly oil the grates.

Place the steaks on the grill over direct heat and cook, uncovered, turning once, until a deep crust forms and the internal temperature reaches your desired doneness:

Rare: 4 to 5 minutes per side (120°F to 125°F [49°C to 51.6°C])

Medium rare: 5 to 6 minutes per side (130°F to 135°F [54°C to 57°C])

Medium: 6 to 7 minutes per side (140°F to 145°F [60°C to 63°C])

Medium well: 7 to 8 minutes per side (150°F to 155°F [65.5°C to 68°C])

GRILLING TIMES FOR OTHER PROTEINS

(TIMES APPROXIMATE, BASED ON MEDIUM-HIGH DIRECT HEAT)

Boneless, skinless chicken breast (6 to 8 ounces [170 to 225 g]):
6 to 8 minutes per side (165°F [74°C])

Boneless, skinless chicken thigh: 5 to 6 minutes per side (165°F [74°C])

Bone-in chicken thigh or drumstick: 10 to 12 minutes per side (165°F [74°C])

Lamb: Lamb chop (1 inch [2.5 cm]):
3 to 4 minutes per side (135°F [57°C] for medium-rare)

Pork chop, boneless (1 inch [2.5 cm]): 4 to 5 minutes per side (145°F [63°C])

Pork tenderloin: 15 to 20 minutes total, turning occasionally (145°F [63°C])

FISH AND SEAFOOD

Salmon fillet (1 inch [2.5 cm]):
4 to 5 minutes per side (125°F to 130°F [52°C to 54°C])

Scallops: 2 to 3 minutes per side (opaque, slightly firm)

Shrimp (large): 2 to 3 minutes per side (opaque throughout)

Whole fish (1 to 2 pounds [450 to 900 g]):
8 to 10 minutes per side (140°F [60°C])

VEGETABLES

Asparagus: 3 to 4 minutes total

Bell pepper (halved): 4 to 5 minutes per side

Corn (husked): 10 to 12 minutes total, turning often

Portobello mushroom: 4 to 5 minutes per side

Zucchini (sliced lengthwise): 3 to 4 minutes per side

Blues don't follow the rules; they follow results. A meal without its accompaniments isn't a meal. It's a missed opportunity.

5

STRATEGIC ACCOMPANIMENTS

Though often dismissed as less important than the leading pair, the dragons and riders who fly in formation as seconds carry the survival of the wing on their backs. They hold the line, reinforce the vulnerable, and strike where least expected.

—*Colonel Kaori's* Field Guide to Dragonkind

Every rider knows the value of a strong second: someone steady at your side when the sky darkens and the odds tilt out of your favor. These dishes may not lead the charge, but they're built to bolster.

Whether blistered by flame, rich with complex flavor, or simply holding everything together, these sides bring reinforcement. They're the dependable ones, the kind of food that doesn't need the spotlight to make the meal.

Choose wisely. A good second can turn the tide—or make the meal.

YIELDS
ABOUT 20 WHEELS

SPINNING
GARLIC PARMESAN WHEELS

Inspired by the brutal first ascent of the Gauntlet, where cadets face a 15-foot (4.5 m) spinning log, soaring granite pillars, and a rotating wheel with only one shot at entry, these savory pinwheels pay homage to the disorienting chaos that kicks off Basgiath's most feared obstacle. But unlike the real thing, these golden swirls of garlic, butter, and Parmesan are impossible to fail . . . unless you forget to share.

- All-purpose flour, for dusting
- 1 sheet frozen puff pastry (from a 1¼-pound [567 g] box containing 2 sheets), thawed but still cold
- ¼ cup (56 g) unsalted butter, at room temperature
- 4 garlic cloves, minced
- 1 tablespoon (4 g) finely chopped fresh parsley
- 1 tablespoon (6.25 g) grated Parmesan cheese
- ¼ teaspoon (0.8 g) kosher salt
- 1 large egg
- 1 tablespoon (15 ml) water

Preheat the oven to 400°F (200°C, or gas mark 6). Line two baking sheets with parchment paper.

Lightly dust a work surface with flour and unfold the puff pastry sheet on it.

In a small bowl, stir together the butter, garlic, parsley, Parmesan, and salt until smooth. In another small bowl, whisk together the egg and water to make the egg wash.

Spread the garlic butter evenly over the puff pastry sheet. Starting at a short side, roll up the pastry tightly into a log, jelly-roll style. Transfer the log to the freezer for 10 minutes, or up to 1 hour, to firm up for easier slicing.

Using a sharp knife, cut the log crosswise into slices ½ inch (1 cm) thick (you should get about twenty). Arrange the slices, cut-side up, on the prepared baking sheets, spacing them about 2 inches (5 cm) apart. Brush the tops with the egg wash.

Bake for about 15 minutes, or until puffed and golden brown. Let cool for 5 minutes before serving. Serve warm.

YIELDS
6 SERVINGS

DAGGERTAIL ROOT ROAST

Only a dragon as formidable as Sgaeyl could inspire a side this bold. Purple potatoes and red cabbage deepen in flavor as they roast, while red onion brings just enough bite to balance the sweetness. Crisped edges and a hit of Parm. Smoky blues that mirror the daggertail's own stormy palette. This dish doesn't ask for compliments. It demands them.

- 3 tablespoons (45 ml) extra-virgin olive oil, divided
- 3 pounds (1.4 kg) purple potatoes, peeled and cut into 1-inch (2.5 cm) cubes
- ½ head red cabbage, cored and cut into 1-inch (2.5 cm) chunks
- 1 red onion, cut into 1-inch (2.5 cm) chunks
- 1 tablespoon (1.7 g) finely chopped fresh rosemary leaves
- 1 teaspoon (3.3 g) kosher salt
- ¼ teaspoon (0.75 g) freshly cracked black pepper
- ¼ cup (25 g) freshly grated Parmesan cheese

Preheat the oven to 450°F (230°C, or gas mark 8). Drizzle 1 tablespoon (15 ml) of the olive oil onto a rimmed baking sheet and use a paper towel to coat the surface evenly.

In a large bowl, combine the potatoes, cabbage, and onion. Drizzle with the remaining 2 tablespoons (30 ml) olive oil, then add the rosemary, salt, and pepper. Toss until coated evenly.

Spread the vegetables in a single layer on the prepared baking sheet, arranging as many as possible flat-side down for optimal browning.

Roast for 20 minutes. Remove the pan from the oven and use a spatula to flip the vegetables. Continue to roast for 15 to 20 minutes more, or until the potatoes are fork-tender and the vegetables are deeply golden brown at the edges.

Remove from the oven and immediately sprinkle the Parmesan over the top. Serve warm.

YIELDS
6 SERVINGS

VIDIRYS CAULIFLOWER STUFFING

At a dinner in the gleaming cream-stoned capital of Hedotis, Violet and the team sit down to a meal that's memorable not for its warmth but for the tension hanging in the air. This hearty cauliflower stuffing, mentioned in Onyx Storm, *was served as part of that uneasy feast. Roasted cauliflower, herbs, and golden bread crumbs come together for a side that's rich, satisfying, . . . and maybe just a little suspicious.*

- 1 large head cauliflower, cut into small florets
- 1 large yellow onion, diced
- ½ cup (60 g) diced celery
- 2 garlic cloves, minced
- ¼ cup (60 ml) extra-virgin olive oil
- 2 teaspoons (3 g) poultry seasoning
- 1 teaspoon (3.3 g) kosher salt
- ¼ teaspoon (0.75 g) freshly ground black pepper
- ¼ cup (13 g) dried breadcrumbs (such as panko)
- 1 tablespoon (14 g) unsalted butter, melted
- 2 tablespoons (8 g) chopped fresh parsley

Preheat the oven to 425°F (220°C, or gas mark 7). Line a large baking sheet with parchment paper.

In a large bowl, combine the cauliflower, onion, celery, and garlic. Add the olive oil, poultry seasoning, salt, and pepper. Toss until everything is coated evenly. Spread the mixture in a single layer on the prepared baking sheet. Use two sheets, if needed, to avoid overcrowding. Arrange the cauliflower and onion pieces cut-side down as much as possible for better browning.

Roast for 15 minutes, or until the onion is softened and the cauliflower is beginning to brown at the edges.

In a small bowl, stir together the bread crumbs and melted butter.

Remove the baking sheet from the oven and sprinkle the bread crumb mixture evenly over the vegetables. Continue to roast for 10 to 15 minutes more, or until the bread crumbs are golden and toasted, the cauliflower is deeply browned, and the onion is starting to caramelize.

Sprinkle with the parsley and serve warm.

YIELDS
4 SERVINGS

FLAME-KISSED CORN ON THE COB

At Basgiath, even the simplest foods feel touched by fire. This corn on the cob, lightly charred and slathered in a garlic-lime-paprika butter, tastes like something you might grab after a long flight lesson. Sweet, savory, and just a little bit zesty, it's a side dish that carries the spirit of the Quadrant: fierce, bright, and a little unpredictable. Best alongside Varrish's "Weak Point" Glazed Ribs (page 77).

½ cup (113 g) salted butter, at room temperature

3 garlic cloves, minced

Grated zest and juice of 1 lime

½ teaspoon (1.15 g) smoked paprika

¼ teaspoon (0.8 g) kosher salt

4 ears of corn, husked and silks removed

1 to 2 tablespoons neutral oil, for oiling the grates (if using a grill)

In a small bowl, combine the butter, garlic, lime zest, lime juice, smoked paprika, and salt. Stir until well mixed and smooth. Set aside.

To grill the corn, preheat a grill to medium-high heat and brush the grill grates clean. Lightly oil the grates, then place the corn on the grill over direct heat. Cook, turning occasionally, until the kernels are tender and charred in spots, 15 to 20 minutes.

To roast the corn in the oven, preheat the oven to 425°F (220°C, or gas mark 7). Line a rimmed baking sheet with aluminum foil or parchment paper.

Place the corn on the prepared baking sheet. Roast for 20 to 25 minutes, turning halfway through, until tender and golden brown in places.

Remove from the grill or oven and brush generously with the garlic-lime butter while hot. Serve warm, with extra butter on the side if desired.

YIELDS
4 SERVINGS

"BETTER THAN YOU THINK"

BROCCOLI WITH FETA AND SHALLOTS

"No one really wants broccoli, but it's good for you, so seems fitting to me." That's what Drake Cordella says when asked why he named his flame-colored kitten Broccoli. While the logic isn't exactly sound, the sentiment fits this dish perfectly. Charred until crisp edged and nutty from toasted sesame, the broccoli is tossed in a sharp lemon-shallot dressing that cuts through the richness of a creamy whipped-feta base. The result is bold, salty, tangy, and far more addictive than it has any right to be, just like the kitten himself.

BROCCOLI

Nonstick cooking spray, for the baking sheet

2 tablespoons (30 ml) extra-virgin olive oil

2 tablespoons (30 ml) soy sauce

2 teaspoons (10 ml) sesame oil

2 pounds (900 g) fresh broccoli florets (from 1 large head)

1 tablespoon (8 g) toasted sesame seeds

WHIPPED FETA

1 (8-ounce, or 225 g) block feta cheese, drained

¾ cup (180 g) plain Greek yogurt

Grated zest of 1 lemon

2 tablespoons (30 ml) extra-virgin olive oil, plus more as needed

LEMON-SHALLOT DRESSING

⅓ cup (80 ml) extra-virgin olive oil

1 small shallot, finely chopped (about ¼ cup, or 40 g)

2 garlic cloves, minced

Juice of 1 lemon

1 tablespoon (15 g) Dijon mustard

½ teaspoon (1.65 g) kosher salt

½ teaspoon (1.5 g) freshly ground black pepper

Preheat the oven to 450°F (230°C, or gas mark 8). Lightly coat a large baking sheet with cooking spray.

To make the broccoli: In a large bowl, whisk together the olive oil, soy sauce, and sesame oil. Add the broccoli and toss until coated evenly. Arrange the florets in a single layer on the prepared baking sheet, placing them flat-side down as much as when possible for better browning.

Roast for 10 minutes. Stir or flip the broccoli and continue to roast for 5 minutes more, or until tender-crisp and browned at the edges. Sprinkle with the sesame seeds and set aside.

To make the whipped feta: While the broccoli cooks, in a food processor fitted with the blade attachment, combine the feta, Greek yogurt, and lemon zest. Blend until smooth. With the processor running, drizzle in the olive oil until fully incorporated and the mixture is light and creamy. Add more olive oil to loosen the texture if needed. Set aside.

To make the lemon-shallot dressing: In a small bowl, whisk together the olive oil, shallot, garlic, lemon juice, mustard, salt, and pepper until combined fully.

To serve, spread the whipped feta onto a serving platter. Top with the warm roasted broccoli and drizzle with the lemon-shallot dressing. Serve immediately.

YIELDS 1 LOAF
(12 TO 16 PIECES)

STONE TABLE BREAD WITH ROSEMARY AND SEA SALT

In Navarre, not every meal is a feast, but there's always bread. This focaccia-inspired loaf is the kind you'd find torn apart at a stone table in the valley, passed between calloused hands and eaten while armor clinks and ash still lingers in the air. Rich with extra-virgin olive oil and topped with rosemary and flaky sea salt, it's golden on the bottom, airy inside, and just herbaceous enough to cut through exhaustion. Serve warm with salted butter, stew, or nothing at all.

2 teaspoons (6.2 g) active dry yeast

1 teaspoon (4 g) granulated sugar

2 cups (475 ml) lukewarm water, about 100°F (38°C)

4 cups (480 g) all-purpose flour

1 tablespoon (10 g) kosher salt

6 tablespoons (90 ml) extra-virgin olive oil, divided

2 teaspoons (1.2 g) finely chopped fresh rosemary leaves

Flaky sea salt (such as Maldon)

JESINIA'S MARGIN NOTES

Let cool completely before storing—residual heat invites unwanted moisture. Once cooled, place in an airtight container and keep at room temperature for up to 3 days. For longer preservation, freeze (properly sealed, of course) for up to 3 months. Future you will be grateful.

In a large bowl, whisk together the yeast, sugar, and lukewarm water. Let sit for 5 to 10 minutes, until foamy, to activate. In another large bowl, whisk together the flour and salt.

Add the dry ingredients to the wet ingredients and mix with a rubber spatula until mostly combined. Use your hands to knead briefly in the bowl until no dry flour remains.

Rub the surface of the dough lightly with about 2 tablespoons (30 ml) of the olive oil. Cover tightly with plastic wrap and let rise at room temperature for 1½ to 2 hours, or until doubled in size.

Grease a 9-by-13-inch (23 by 33 cm) glass baking dish with 2 tablespoons (30 ml) of the olive oil. Transfer the dough to the dish and turn once or twice to coat in the oil. Let rest, uncovered, at room temperature for 30 minutes, or until puffy and visibly risen.

Preheat the oven to 425°F (220°C, or gas mark 7).

Sprinkle the rosemary evenly over the surface of the dough. Drizzle with the remaining 2 tablespoons (30 ml) olive oil. Press your fingertips straight down into the dough to create deep dimples across the surface. If needed, gently stretch the dough to fill the dish as you dimple. Sprinkle generously with sea salt.

Bake for 25 to 30 minutes, or until the bottom is crisp and golden brown. Transfer the focaccia to a wire rack and let cool for 10 minutes before slicing and serving.

YIELDS
4 SERVINGS

EMBERED
POTATO PACKETS

When you're camped along the outskirts of enemy territory, or just out on a scouting mission, nothing beats the comfort of potatoes roasted in the embers of a dying fire (or perhaps quickly seared by dragon flame). These foil-wrapped bundles, packed with tender potatoes, charred onions, smoky seasoning, and a dusting of Parmesan, feel like the kind of meal riders might tuck in to during a long night patrol alongside Violent Little Kebabs (page 72) or "Marked by Flame" Grilled Steak with Rosemary Marinade (page 92).

- 2 pounds (900 g) Yukon gold or red potatoes, cut into ¼-inch (0.6 cm) slices
- 1 small yellow onion, thinly sliced
- 1 tablespoon (15 ml) extra-virgin olive oil
- 1½ teaspoons (5 g) kosher salt
- 1 teaspoon (2.3 g) smoked paprika
- ½ teaspoon (1.5 g) garlic powder
- ¼ teaspoon (0.75 g) freshly ground black pepper
- 4 tablespoons (25 g) grated Parmesan cheese

If baking, preheat the oven to 375°F (190°C, or gas mark 5).

If grilling, preheat a grill to medium heat and brush the grill grates clean.

If cooking over a campfire, let the flames burn down to glowing embers.

Cut four 12-by-18-inch (30 by 45 cm) sheets of aluminum foil.

In a large bowl, combine the potatoes, onion, olive oil, salt, paprika, garlic powder, and pepper. Toss until coated evenly. Divide the mixture evenly among the foil sheets, placing it in the center of each. Sprinkle each with about 1 tablespoon (6.25 g) of the Parmesan.

To seal the packets, bring the long sides of the foil together and fold over tightly, then fold in the ends to form a secure pouch. A small gap is fine—steam needs somewhere to go.

To bake: Place the foil packets on a baking sheet and bake for 25 to 30 minutes, or until the potatoes are tender when pierced with a fork.

To grill: Place the packets directly on the grill over direct heat and cook for 25 to 30 minutes, or until the potatoes are tender when pierced with a fork.

To cook over a campfire: Nestle the packets among the hot embers (not in direct flames). Cook, rotating the packets occasionally, for 25 to 30 minutes, or until the potatoes are fork-tender.

Carefully open the packets—watch out for steam—and serve straight from the foil or spoon onto plates.

YIELDS
4 SERVINGS

SHAKING PILLAR

VEGGIE SKEWERS

In the third ascent of the Gauntlet, cadets must swing bar to bar, building momentum before leaping onto unstable iron pillars. While these veggie skewers aren't stacked as precariously, each bite delivers a similar balance of tension and triumph. Grilled over an open flame or roasted under a broiler, these vegetable stacks bring smoky-sweet depth from charred sweet potatoes and earthy mushrooms, brightness from bell peppers and red onion, and a final punch of garlicky herb sauce that clings to every edge. The result is a side dish alive with flame and flavor.

VEGETABLE SKEWERS

1 large sweet potato, cut into 1-inch (2.5 cm) cubes

4 to 6 baby red potatoes, cut into 1-inch (2.5 cm) cubes

1 medium red bell pepper, cut into 1-inch (2.5 cm) pieces

1 medium yellow bell pepper, cut into 1-inch (2.5 cm) pieces

1 medium red onion, cut into 1-inch (2.5 cm) pieces

2 large portobello mushrooms, wiped clean and cut into 1-inch (2.5 cm) pieces

2 tablespoons (30 ml) extra-virgin olive oil, divided

½ teaspoon (1.65 g) kosher salt

¼ teaspoon (0.75 g) freshly ground black pepper

GARLIC HERB SAUCE

⅓ cup (80 ml) extra-virgin olive oil

5 garlic cloves, minced

3 tablespoons (12 g) chopped fresh parsley

3 tablespoons (3 g) chopped fresh cilantro

1 teaspoon (0.6 g) chopped fresh rosemary leaves

Kosher salt and freshly ground black pepper

Preheat a grill to medium and brush the grill grates clean. Alternatively, preheat the broiler, using the high setting if available. If using wooden skewers, soak them in water for 30 minutes to prevent burning. Line a broiler pan or baking sheet with aluminum foil if using the broiler.

To make the vegetable skewers: Place the sweet potatoes and red potatoes in a large pot and cover with water. Bring to a boil over high heat and cook for 8 to 10 minutes, or until barely fork-tender. Drain and let cool slightly.

Thread the sweet potatoes, red potatoes, bell peppers, onion, and mushrooms onto metal (or soaked wooden) skewers, leaving space at each end for easier flipping. Brush all over with 1 tablespoon (15 ml) of the olive oil and season with the salt and pepper.

Place the skewers on the grill over direct heat or in the prepared broiler pan. Cook for 10 to 15 minutes, flipping halfway through, until the vegetables are tender and charred in spots. If browning too quickly, reduce the heat or move the skewers to a cooler area of the grill or farther away from the heating element of the broiler.

To make the garlic herb sauce: While the vegetables cook, in a medium bowl, whisk together the olive oil, garlic, parsley, cilantro, rosemary, and salt and pepper to taste.

Brush the cooked skewers generously with the garlic herb sauce. Serve warm.

"Marbh always did have a taste for something sweet at the end. Can't say I blame him."

—B. S.

6

SWEETS AND SMALL INDULGENCES

The boundary between medicinal herb and fatal toxin is narrow and often sweetened. Custards conceal bitter tinctures, tarts mask fermented death. Always know your ingredients. And who you're sourcing them from.

—Effective Uses of Wild and Cultivated Herbs *by Captain Lawrence Medina*

Whether you've just bonded a dragon, survived a sparring match, or narrowly avoided death by berry tart, these treats offer a moment of softness in a world that rarely allows it. But make no mistake: These aren't your average comfort foods.

Every dessert in this collection carries a little power and a lot of personality. From blistered peaches to iridescent lemon bars, each recipe speaks to a deeper story from The Empyrean series—a stolen moment of pleasure, an offering of trust, or a reminder that sweetness can be as strategic as any weapon.

These are indulgences you'll be willing to fight for. Best enjoyed late at night, shared with your squad, or hoarded like a secret worth keeping.

YIELDS
8 SERVINGS

XADEN'S CHOCOLATE CAKE

In a world where trust is currency, Xaden Riorson keeps his vulnerabilities well guarded . . . except, perhaps, when it comes to chocolate cake. Mentioned more than once throughout the series and brought to life in Onyx Storm *by a ghost from Xaden's past, this cake leans all the way in: rich with dark cocoa, deepened by hot coffee, and stacked high with classic chocolate buttercream.*

CAKE

Nonstick cooking spray, for the cake pans
2¼ cups (270 g) all-purpose flour
1 cup (80 g) unsweetened cocoa powder
2 teaspoons (9.2 g) baking soda
1 teaspoon (4.6 g) baking powder
1 teaspoon (3.3 g) kosher salt
⅓ cup (80 ml) vegetable oil
1 cup (240 g) sour cream, at room temperature
½ cup (113 g) unsalted butter, at room temperature
2 cups (400 g) granulated sugar
½ cup (113 g) packed light brown sugar
3 large eggs, at room temperature
2 teaspoons (10 ml) pure vanilla extract
1 cup (240 ml) freshly brewed hot coffee

FROSTING

1½ cups (339 g) unsalted butter, at room temperature
5 cups (560 g) powdered sugar, plus more as needed
¾ cup (60 g) unsweetened cocoa powder
¼ cup (60 ml) whole milk, plus more as needed
¼ teaspoon (0.8 g) kosher salt, plus more as needed
1 tablespoon (15 ml) pure vanilla extract

Preheat the oven to 350°F (180°C, or gas mark 4). Coat two 9-inch (23 cm) round cake pans with cooking spray.

To make the cake: In a large bowl, whisk together the flour, cocoa powder, baking soda, baking powder, and salt. In a medium bowl, stir together the vegetable oil and sour cream. Set the bowls aside.

In the bowl of a stand mixer fitted with the paddle attachment, or in a large bowl with a hand mixer, beat the butter on medium until smooth, about 1 minute. Gradually add the granulated and brown sugars, beating well and scraping down the bowl as needed. Increase to high and beat until light and fluffy, about 4 minutes. Beat in the eggs one at a time, then the vanilla, until fully incorporated.

Reduce the mixer speed to low. Add the flour mixture in three additions, alternating with the sour cream mixture and beginning and ending with the dry ingredients. Beat just until incorporated after each addition—do not overmix.

Fold in the hot coffee with a spatula just until combined. The batter will be loose. Divide the batter evenly between the prepared pans and smooth the tops.

Bake for 35 to 45 minutes, or until a toothpick inserted into the center comes out clean or with a few moist crumbs.

Cool the cakes in the pans on a wire rack for 20 minutes. Invert the cakes onto the rack and let cool completely, about 1 hour.

To make the frosting: Using the stand or hand mixer, beat the butter on medium speed until creamy, about 2 minutes. Add the powdered sugar, cocoa, milk, salt, and vanilla. Mix on low for 30 seconds, then beat on high for 1 minute. Adjust the consistency with more powdered sugar to thicken or milk to thin. Season with extra salt if desired.

To assemble: Place one cake layer on a plate or stand and spread a generous layer of frosting over the top. Add the second layer, then frost the top and sides.

For a Xaden-approved finish, use a star or petal tip to pipe jagged peaks, evoking shadowed terrain or dagger points. Slice and serve.

Continues on page 113

JESINIA'S MARGIN NOTES

Not a coffee drinker? No need to brew an entire pot. Dissolve a packet of instant coffee in hot water to produce the small amount needed. Efficient, unobtrusive, and unlikely to awaken any long-dormant caffeine habits.

"ZAKIA BERRY" FILLING (OPTIONAL)

There's nothing sweet about zakia berries—but there is about this filling. In Onyx Storm, *they nearly ended Garrick's life and pushed Xaden to the edge of himself. But that night in Vidirys was also when Violet proved she'd risk everything for the people she loves, even if it meant turning poison into leverage.*

This optional filling takes inspiration from that moment: tart raspberries (our stand-in for zakia berries) cooked into a jammy, punchy sauce that cuts straight through the cake's chocolate intensity. At first it might seem like it doesn't belong here, but neither did betrayal at a table set with chocolate cake.

Enclose it between the layers if you want your dessert to carry a little danger. Just keep your friends close—and your antidotes closer.

¼ cup (50 g) granulated sugar

4 teaspoons (10.6 g) cornstarch

1 tablespoon (15 ml) water

1 tablespoon (15 ml) freshly squeezed lemon juice

2 cups (250 g) fresh raspberries, or (300 g) frozen, plus fresh raspberries, for topping (optional)

In a medium saucepan over medium heat, stir together the sugar, cornstarch, water, and lemon juice until smooth. Add the raspberries and cook, stirring often, until the fruit breaks down and the mixture thickens, 6 to 8 minutes. The filling should coat the back of a spoon. Remove from the heat and let cool completely.

To use, spread the raspberry filling over the first cake layer, then top with a thin layer of frosting. Continue with assembly as directed in the main cake recipe.

Top the finished cake with fresh raspberries, if desired.

YIELDS
4 SERVINGS

"VILADRITE" LAVENDER LEMON PANNA COTTA

This silky lavender panna cotta pays homage to mineral-rich Hedotis, where the rare element viladrite seeps into everything, gradually turning pale eyes violet. Beneath its smooth surface lies a sharp lemon curd layered with a floral lavender cream for the perfect contrast. The result is elegant, for sure. But like Hedotis itself, there's danger in the beauty. Trust it too quickly, and you'll miss the bite beneath the bloom.

LEMON CURD

1 tablespoon (6 g) grated lemon zest

⅓ cup (80 ml) freshly squeezed lemon juice

½ cup (100 g) granulated sugar

½ cup (113 g) unsalted butter, cut into pieces

2 large eggs

2 large egg yolks

LAVENDER PANNA COTTA

2½ cups (600 ml) heavy cream

2 tablespoons (3.5 g) dried culinary-grade lavender buds, plus more for garnish

⅓ cup (80 ml) milk (1% or 2%)

One ¼-ounce (7 g) envelope unflavored gelatin

½ cup (100 g) granulated sugar

1½ teaspoons (8 ml) pure vanilla extract

3 to 5 drops purple food coloring

Lemon slices, for garnish (optional)

To make the lemon curd: In a medium saucepan over medium-low heat, whisk together the lemon zest, lemon juice, sugar, butter, eggs, and egg yolks. Cook, whisking constantly, until the mixture thickens enough to hold its shape briefly when dolloped, 7 to 10 minutes. Strain the curd through a fine-mesh sieve into a heat-safe bowl to remove the zest and any curdled bits. Divide the curd evenly among four 8-ounce (240 ml) Mason jars or serving glasses. Refrigerate until chilled and set, about 1 hour.

To make the lavender panna cotta: While the curd chills, in a medium saucepan over medium heat, warm the heavy cream, stirring frequently, 3 to 5 minutes. Add the lavender and remove from the heat. Cover and let steep for 15 minutes.

In a small bowl, stir together the milk and gelatin until the gelatin is dissolved fully. Set aside.

Strain the lavender cream through a fine-mesh sieve into a bowl to remove the lavender buds. Return the strained cream to the saucepan and add the sugar. Place the pan over medium heat and bring to a low boil, stirring constantly. Stir in the milk-gelatin mixture and continue to cook for 1 minute, stirring until dissolved fully. Remove from the heat and stir in the vanilla and enough food coloring to tint the mixture a light purple.

Let the mixture cool to room temperature, about 20 minutes. Gently pour it over the chilled lemon curd in each jar, dividing evenly.

Cover the jars with plastic wrap or lids and refrigerate until fully set, at least 4 hours or up to overnight.

Before serving, garnish with dried lavender buds and lemon slices (if using). Serve cold.

JESINIA'S MARGIN NOTES

Edible pressed violets can be elusive in local markets, but they're readily available online. I suggest acquiring more than needed—some may arrive imperfect, and others are simply too lovely not to keep for correspondence sealing, gift wrapping, or . . . more cookies.

YIELDS
ABOUT 30 COOKIES

VIOLET'S VANILLA SHORTBREAD COOKIES

Violets are delicate: thin as parchment, easily bruised, and often underestimated—much like Violet Sorrengail. But layer them over a buttery shortbread laced with rosemary and finished with a vanilla glaze and the effect is anything but fragile. Just like the rider they're named for, these cookies are built to survive worse than a warm kitchen. In fact, call them fragile again. See what happens.

SHORTBREAD COOKIES

⅔ cup (133 g) granulated sugar

⅓ cup (37 g) powdered sugar

1 teaspoon (3.3 g) kosher salt

1 cup (226 g) unsalted butter, at room temperature

2 large egg yolks

2 teaspoons (10 ml) pure vanilla extract

2 cups (240 g) all-purpose flour

½ cup (96 g) sanding sugar or other coarse sugar

2 teaspoons (1.2 g) finely chopped fresh rosemary leaves

VANILLA BEAN GLAZE

½ cup (120 ml) whole milk, plus more as needed

1 vanilla bean

5 cups (560 g) powdered sugar, sifted, plus more as needed

Pinch of kosher salt

Dried pressed culinary-grade violets, for decorating

To make the shortbread cookies: In a medium bowl, whisk together the granulated sugar, powdered sugar, and salt.

In the bowl of a stand mixer fitted with the paddle attachment, or in a large bowl using a hand mixer, beat the butter on medium speed until creamy, about 1 minute. Add the sugar mixture and beat until light and fluffy, 2 to 3 minutes. Scrape down the sides of the bowl. Mix in the egg yolks and vanilla on low until combined.

On low speed, gradually add the flour until just combined; do not overmix. On a lightly floured surface, pat the dough into a 4-by-6-inch (10 by 15 cm) rectangle. Halve lengthwise to form two 2-by-6-inch (5 by 15 cm) strips. Roll each half into a log 2 inches (5 cm) thick and 6 to 7 inches (15 to 18 cm) long.

In a small shallow bowl, stir together the sanding sugar and rosemary. Roll each dough log in the sugar mixture, pressing gently to adhere. Wrap each log tightly in plastic wrap and refrigerate until firm, at least 2 hours or up to overnight.

Preheat the oven to 350°F (180°C, or gas mark 4). Line three baking sheets with parchment paper.

Unwrap the dough and slice the logs into rounds ½ inch (1 cm) thick. Arrange the rounds 2 inches (5 cm) apart on the prepared baking sheets.

Bake for 14 to 16 minutes, or until the edges are lightly golden and the centers are still pale. Let the cookies cool on the pans on wire racks for 5 minutes, then transfer to the wire racks to cool completely.

To make the vanilla bean glaze: While the cookies cool, pour the milk into a cup or small bowl. Split the vanilla bean lengthwise and scrape the seeds into the milk. Let steep for 15 minutes.

In a medium bowl, whisk together the powdered sugar, salt, and vanilla-infused milk. Add more milk or powdered sugar as needed to achieve a pourable glaze consistency. Whisk until smooth.

Dip the cooled cookie tops into the glaze, then press in the violets. Let sit for 30 minutes. Store in an airtight container at room temperature for up to 3 days.

YIELDS 4 SERVINGS

DAIN'S CRACKED LOYALTY CRÈME BRÛLÉE

This crème brûlée holds fast to its structure . . . until it doesn't. Just like a certain codex-quoting wingleader whose principles were built on rules and eventually broken by the truth of who he trusted (and who he shouldn't have). The crisp caramelized top cracks to reveal a custard laced with chai: warm, spiced, and more complicated than it first seems. Serve to friends you haven't spoken to in a while. Just maybe don't touch their faces.

2 cups (475 ml) heavy cream

1 vanilla bean, split lengthwise, or 1 teaspoon (5 ml) pure vanilla extract

2 black tea bags

½ teaspoon (1.3 g) ground cinnamon

¼ teaspoon (0.50 g) ground cardamom

¼ teaspoon (0.4 g) ground ginger

⅛ teaspoon (0.4 g) kosher salt

5 large egg yolks

½ cup (100 g) granulated sugar

4 tablespoons (60 g) raw sugar, divided

Preheat the oven to 325°F (170°C, or gas mark 3).

In a medium saucepan over low heat, combine the heavy cream, vanilla bean, tea bags, cinnamon, cardamom, ginger, and salt. Warm until hot but not boiling, about 5 minutes. Remove from the heat and let steep for 5 minutes.

Strain the milk mixture through a fine-mesh sieve into a heat-safe bowl, discarding the solids. Set aside to cool slightly.

Bring a medium pot of water to a boil over high heat.

In a medium bowl, whisk the egg yolks and granulated sugar until pale and slightly thickened. Slowly whisk in about ¼ cup (60 ml) of the warm cream to temper the eggs. Gradually add the remaining cream, whisking constantly until combined fully.

Place four 6-ounce (180 ml) broiler-proof ramekins in a deep baking dish. Divide the custard evenly among the ramekins. Carefully pour the boiling water into the baking dish around the ramekins until it reaches halfway up the sides of the ramekins, taking care not to get any water into the custards.

Bake for 30 to 40 minutes, or until the custard centers are just set, with a slight jiggle. Remove the ramekins from the water bath and let cool to room temperature. Cover and refrigerate for at least 4 hours or up to 2 days.

When ready to serve, position an oven rack in the highest position in the oven and preheat the broiler, using the high setting if available. Sprinkle 1 tablespoon (15 g) of the raw sugar over each custard in a thin, even layer. Place the ramekins on a baking sheet, slide under the broiler, and broil for 3 to 5 minutes, or until the sugar melts and caramelizes, watching carefully to avoid burning.

Let the crème brûlées sit for a few minutes so the tops harden. Serve within 2 hours.

YIELDS
4 SERVINGS

DRAGONFIRE PEACHES WITH HONEY, PISTACHIOS, AND ICE CREAM

These peaches don't just get roasted—they get scorched. Whether seared on the grill or broiled until their edges blister and caramelize, they're a fiery nod to dragonkind. Finished with honey, spiced pistachios, and a cold scoop of vanilla ice cream, they strike the perfect balance between searing eat and soothing cool. It's the kind of dessert you'd expect at a post-battle feast or during a late-night rendezvous between squadmates who might be up to more than just sparring.

4 ripe peaches, halved and pitted

Extra-virgin olive oil, for brushing

½ cup (70 g) roasted, shelled pistachios, roughly chopped

2 tablespoons (28 g) salted butter, melted

1 tablespoon (20 g) honey, plus more for drizzling

½ teaspoon (1.3 g) ground cinnamon

¼ teaspoon (0.8 g) kosher salt

Vanilla ice cream, for serving

Preheat a grill to medium heat and brush the grill grates clean or place a grill pan over medium heat on the stovetop. Alternatively, preheat the broiler, using the high setting if available, and line a rimmed baking sheet with aluminum foil.

Brush the cut sides of the peaches lightly with olive oil.

If grilling, place the peaches cut-side down on the grill over direct heat, or in the grill pan, and cook for about 3 minutes, or until char marks appear.

If broiling, place the peaches, cut-side up, on the prepared baking sheet and broil for 2 to 3 minutes, or until browned and bubbling, watching closely to prevent burning.

In a small bowl, stir together the pistachios, melted butter, honey, cinnamon, and salt until well combined.

Remove the peaches from the grill, pan, or broiler.

To serve, place two halves in each bowl, spoon the pistachio mixture over the top, add a scoop of vanilla ice cream, and drizzle with honey. Serve immediately.

JESINIA'S MARGIN NOTES

To halve and pit peaches cleanly, use a paring knife to slice along the natural seam, top to bottom. Twist the halves gently in opposite directions to separate. For the pit: Needle-nose pliers are surprisingly effective. Grip, twist, and lift with care (a technique I first observed during a foraging lecture).

YIELDS ABOUT 32 COOKIES

DRAGON-SCALE COOKIES

Delicate and green, these crisp lace cookies are inspired by Teine, Mira's green clubtail, and the lovingly passive-aggressive gift of a scale-armored vest Mira gives Violet. Because nothing says "I believe in you" like wrapping your little sister in reptilian Kevlar and sending her off to dodge death with a smile. Bake these when you want to impress, intimidate, or insulate someone you love. Preferably all three.

- 1 cup (226 g) unsalted butter
- 1½ cups (300 g) granulated sugar
- 2 large eggs, beaten
- 1 teaspoon (5 ml) pure vanilla extract
- 2 cups (160 g) quick-cooking rolled oats
- ⅓ cup (40 g) all-purpose flour
- ½ teaspoon (2.3 g) baking powder
- ¼ teaspoon (0.8 g) kosher salt
- 1 drop black food coloring
- 2 or 3 drops green food coloring
- Edible luster powder, for decoration

Preheat the oven to 350°F (180°C, or gas mark 4). Line two baking sheets with parchment paper.

In a large microwave-safe bowl, melt the butter in the microwave. Stir in the sugar until combined fully. Add the beaten eggs and vanilla and mix well. Stir in the oats, flour, baking powder, and salt until incorporated.

Add the black food coloring, then the green food coloring, 1 drop at a time, mixing after each addition, until the dough reaches a vibrant, dark-green hue.

Drop tablespoon-size (about 15 g) spoonfuls of dough onto the prepared baking sheets, spacing them at least 3 inches (7.5 cm) apart. (The cookies will spread significantly.) Bake in batches as needed.

Bake for 8 to 10 minutes, or until the edges are golden brown and the centers are set. Let the cookies cool completely on the baking sheets on wire racks. Once cool, use a small paintbrush to dust the tops with edible luster powder.

Store in an airtight container at room temperature for up to 1 week.

JESINIA'S MARGIN NOTES

The edible luster powder is essential to achieving the proper dragon-scale shimmer. It's entirely worth the effort. Most craft stores carry it, though online vendors offer a broader selection.

As for the dough: Do adhere to the tablespoon-size portions. Though it may seem modest, these cookies spread dramatically in the oven. Much like Teine, they're best when given ample room.

JESINIA'S MARGIN NOTES

Pressed for time? A boxed brownie mix and boxed vanilla pudding in place of the custard will suffice. Although not quite the same as crafting each layer by hand, the spirit of the dish remains intact. Efficiency has its place, especially when the climb is steep.

YIELDS
6 TO 8 SERVINGS

VERTICAL VICTORY
BROWNIE TRIFLE

This layered dessert is a tribute to the final ascent of the Gauntlet: a sheer, vertical climb that separates survivors from legends. Dense brownie cubes form the base, a nod to the ground beneath the leaning chimney. Above that, a silky vanilla custard climbs upward, steady and controlled. A layer of macerated strawberries follows—sweet, streaked, and just a little chaotic, like scraped palms and knees. At the summit, more strawberries spill over the edge, capturing the vivid, hard-won glory of reaching the top. Served in clear glasses to show off every hard-won layer, this one's best enjoyed with a side of triumph . . . or maybe a rope, just in case.

VANILLA CUSTARD

4 cups (950 ml) whole milk
1 tablespoon (15 ml) pure vanilla extract
1 teaspoon (4.6 g) unsalted butter
4 large eggs
½ cup (100 g) granulated sugar
3 tablespoons (24 g) cornstarch

BROWNIES

½ cup (113 g) unsalted butter, melted and slightly cooled
1 cup (200 g) granulated sugar
1 teaspoon (5 ml) pure vanilla extract
2 large eggs
¼ teaspoon (1.15 g) baking soda
¼ teaspoon (0.8 g) kosher salt
½ cup (60 g) all-purpose flour
⅓ cup (40 g) unsweetened cocoa powder
1½ cups (270 g) semisweet chocolate chips

MACERATED STRAWBERRIES

4 cups (580 g) fresh strawberries, hulled and halved
½ cup (100 g) granulated sugar

8 oz (227g) whipped topping, thawed

To make the vanilla custard: In a medium saucepan over medium heat, combine the milk, vanilla, and butter. Bring just to a simmer, then remove from the heat.

In a medium bowl, whisk the eggs, sugar, and cornstarch until the sugar is dissolved and the mixture is smooth.

Return the saucepan to low heat. Slowly pour in the egg mixture, whisking constantly. Continue to cook, whisking, until the custard thickens enough to coat the back of a spoon, 5 to 10 minutes. Transfer the custard to a large bowl. Cover and refrigerate until fully cooled.

Preheat the oven to 350°F (180°C, or gas mark 4). Line a 9-by-9-inch (23 by 23 cm) metal baking pan with parchment paper or aluminum foil.

To make the brownies: In a large bowl, whisk together the melted butter, sugar, and vanilla. Add the eggs and whisk until smooth. Add the baking soda, salt, flour, and cocoa powder. Stir until just combined. Fold in the chocolate chips. The batter will be thick. Spread the batter into the prepared pan.

Bake for 25 to 30 minutes, until the top is set and a toothpick inserted near the center comes out with just a few moist crumbs. Let cool in the pan or on a wire rack for 30 minutes, then cut into 1-inch (2.5 cm) cubes.

To make the macerated strawberries: In a medium saucepan over medium heat, combine the strawberries and sugar. Cook, stirring occasionally, until the berries begin to break down and release their juices, about 10 minutes. Remove from the heat and cool completely.

To assemble the trifle: In a large trifle dish or individual clear glasses, layer the ingredients in the following order: brownies, custard, strawberries, whipped topping. Repeat the layers, then end with strawberries on top.

Chill for at least 1 hour and up to 6 hours before serving.

YIELDS
24 BARS

IRIDESCENT
BLACKBERRY LEMON BARS

Inspired by the elusive Irid dragons, these bars start out simple—then shift into something dazzling. The base is a classic shortbread crust: quiet, steady, grounding. But the custard is where things begin to shimmer. Blackberries deepen the lemon filling into a moodier hue and tarter flavor, while a dusting of edible pearl powder gives the bars an effect worthy of legend. Like the Irid, they're striking, layered, and not to be underestimated.

Nonstick cooking spray or unsalted butter, for the baking dish

CRUST

1½ cups (180 g) all-purpose flour

⅔ cup (75 g) powdered sugar

¾ cup (168 g) cold unsalted butter, cut into ½-inch (1 cm) cubes

BLACKBERRY-LEMON CUSTARD

2 cups (290 g) fresh blackberries, or 2 cups (320 g) frozen

2 cups (400 g) granulated sugar, divided

8 large eggs

1 cup (240 ml) freshly squeezed lemon juice (from 4 large lemons)

½ cup (60 g) all-purpose flour

Edible pearlescent powder, for dusting

Preheat the oven to 375°F (190°C, or gas mark 5). Lightly grease a 9-by-13-inch (23 by 33 cm) glass baking dish with cooking spray.

To make the crust: In the bowl of a stand mixer, or in a large bowl using a fork, mix the flour, powdered sugar, and butter until crumbly and combined evenly. Press the mixture firmly into the bottom of the prepared baking dish.

Bake for 18 to 20 minutes, or until the edges are golden. Remove and leave the oven on.

To make the blackberry-lemon custard: While the crust bakes, in a small saucepan over medium heat, combine the blackberries and ½ cup (100 g) of the granulated sugar. Bring to a simmer, stirring and mashing the berries until they release their juices, 7 to 10 minutes. Strain the mixture through a fine-mesh sieve into a heat-safe bowl. Reserve the strained blackberry juice and discard the solids.

In a large bowl, whisk together the blackberry juice, remaining 1½ cups (300 g) granulated sugar, eggs, lemon juice, and flour until smooth and frothy. Pour the custard over the hot crust. Return the baking dish to the oven and bake for 20 to 25 minutes, or until the center is just set and no longer jiggles when gently shaken.

Let cool at room temperature for at least 20 minutes. Cover and refrigerate for at least 2 hours, or until fully chilled, and up to 3 days.

Just before serving, dust the surface with pearlescent powder for a luminous dragon-scale sheen. Cut into bars and serve cold.

YIELDS
24 TO 30 COOKIES

ANDARNA'S BUTTERSCOTCH CHOCOLATE ECLIPSE COOKIES

Andarna has always defied expectations, from the gold scales of her childhood to her startling shift to inky black (or so we thought), and the truths that each evolution revealed. This cookie channels that duality with a swirl of golden butterscotch and deep cocoa doughs, twisted together like a midair barrel roll. Soft, rich, and a little different, they land somewhere between comfortingly familiar and entirely new, just like our girl.

BUTTERSCOTCH DOUGH

½ cup (113 g) packed light brown sugar
¼ cup (50 g) granulated sugar
½ cup (113 g) unsalted butter, at room temperature
½ teaspoon (2.5 ml) pure vanilla extract
1 large egg
1¼ cups (150 g) all-purpose flour
½ teaspoon (2.3 g) baking soda
½ teaspoon (1.65 g) kosher salt
¼ teaspoon (0.6 g) ground cinnamon
1 cup (180 g) butterscotch chips

CHOCOLATE DOUGH

¾ cup (150 g) granulated sugar
½ cup (113 g) unsalted butter, at room temperature
1 teaspoon (5 ml) pure vanilla extract
1 large egg
1 cup (120 g) all-purpose flour
⅓ cup (27 g) unsweetened cocoa powder
½ teaspoon (2.3 g) baking soda
¼ teaspoon (0.8 g) kosher salt
1 cup (180 g) semisweet chocolate chips
Flaky sea salt

To make the butterscotch dough: In the bowl of a stand mixer fitted with the paddle attachment, or in a large bowl using a hand mixer, beat the brown sugar, granulated sugar, butter, and vanilla on medium speed until light and fluffy, about 2 minutes. Add the egg and beat until smooth.

In a medium bowl, whisk together the flour, baking soda, salt, and cinnamon. With the mixer on low speed, gradually add the dry ingredients to the wet ingredients and mix until just combined. Fold in the butterscotch chips. Set aside.

To make the chocolate dough: In the clean bowl of the stand mixer fitted with the cleaned paddle attachment, or in a clean large bowl and using the hand mixer with cleaned beaters, beat the granulated sugar, butter, vanilla, and egg on medium speed until light and fluffy, about 2 minutes.

In a medium bowl, whisk together the flour, cocoa, baking soda, and salt. On low speed, mix the dry ingredients into the wet ingredients until just combined. Fold in the chocolate chips. The chocolate dough will be drier than the butterscotch.

On a clean surface, pat each dough into a 12-by-8-inch (30 by 20 cm) rectangle about ½ inch (1 cm) thick. Stack one rectangle on top of the other, then roll tightly into a log, starting from a long edge. Wrap the log tightly in plastic wrap and refrigerate until firm, at least 1 hour or up to overnight.

Preheat the oven to 350°F (180°C, or gas mark 4). Line two rimmed baking sheets with parchment paper.

Slice the chilled dough into rounds ½ inch (1 cm) thick and arrange on the prepared baking sheets about 2 inches (5 cm) apart. Sprinkle each cookie with sea salt.

Bake for 12 to 15 minutes, until the centers are set but soft. Cool on the baking sheets for 5 minutes, then transfer to a wire rack to cool completely.

Store in an airtight container at room temperature for up to 3 days.

YIELDS 16 BARS

SCORCHED EARTH
S'MORES BARS

Some desserts comfort, but this one conquers—the potluck table, that is. Built on a graham cracker–crust base and layered with molten chocolate, creamy peanut butter, and blistered marshmallow creme, these bars are just the right amount of unhinged. You won't find them at a polite banquet. They're more likely stashed in a rider's pack, eaten with singed fingers after a night flight or victory that came too close. Sweet, sticky, and way too messy, this is s'mores, Basgiath style.

½ cup (113 g) unsalted butter, at room temperature

½ cup (100 g) granulated sugar

¼ cup (56 g) packed light brown sugar

1 large egg

1 teaspoon (5 ml) pure vanilla extract

1¼ cups (150 g) all-purpose flour

1 teaspoon (4.6 g) baking powder

1 teaspoon (3.3 g) kosher salt

6 graham crackers, crushed into fine crumbs, about 1 cup (120 g)

½ cup (130 g) creamy peanut butter

Four 1.55-ounce (43.9 g) milk chocolate bars

One 7-ounce (200 g) jar marshmallow creme

Preheat the oven to 350°F (180°C, or gas mark 4). Line an 8-by-8-inch (20 by 20 cm) baking dish with parchment paper, allowing the parchment to overlap the sides.

In the bowl of a stand mixer fitted with the paddle attachment, or in a large bowl using a hand mixer, beat the butter, granulated sugar, and brown sugar on medium speed, about 2 to 3 minutes. Add the egg and vanilla and mix until combined fully.

On low speed, add the flour, baking powder, and salt and mix until just incorporated. Add the graham cracker crumbs and mix briefly until distributed evenly. Divide the dough in half. Press one half of the dough evenly into the prepared baking dish. Using the parchment as a sling, lift the dough out of the dish and set aside—this will become the top crust. Line the bottom and sides of the baking dish in the refrigerator before cutting, then lift the dough out using the parchment and transfer it to a cutting board. Press the remaining dough into the bottom of the baking dish.

Gently spread the peanut butter over the dough. Arrange the chocolate bars in a single layer over the peanut butter, breaking as needed to fit. Spoon the marshmallow creme over the chocolate and spread evenly.

Carefully flip the reserved dough layer onto the marshmallow. Peel off the parchment and press gently to flatten.

Bake for 30 minutes, or until the top is golden brown. Let cool completely in the baking dish on a wire rack.

For the cleanest slices, let rest for 4 to 6 hours at room temperature or chill briefly in the refrigerator before cutting. Serve at room temperature.

Store bars in an airtight container at room temperature for up to 3 days, or in the refrigerator for up to 1 week. If refrigerated, allow the bars to reach room temperature before serving for the best texture.

"The feathertails know what heals before you even know you're hurt. We've spent centuries trying to catch up."

(Annotation: This is true. —J)

7

HEALING TINCTURES AND SPIRITED CONCOCTIONS

A well-balanced tincture may soothe pain, steady nerves, or render the subject unconscious within minutes. The outcome depends less on dosage than on intent.

—Major Frederick's Modern Guide for Healers

Not every remedy comes from a mender's belt pouch. Some are poured into copper cups and passed around a fire. Others arrive in crystal coupes at royal banquets.

Whether you need courage before a spar, comfort after a loss, or something strong enough to forget that your dragon is giving you the silent treatment, this collection has you covered.

These cocktails and coolers are as complex as the riders who drink them. Bold, bitter, sweet, and sometimes spiked with more than just alcohol. Just make sure you know what's in your drink. And who handed it to you.

YIELDS
6 TO 8 COCKTAILS

BASGIATH LAVENDER LEMONADE

Served at nearly every post-victory party, this floral lemonade is a staple in the Basgiath courtyard, usually ladled from a too-large metal bowl and spiked without subtlety. This version dials up the drama with Empress 1908 gin, which turns the drink a striking violet hue worthy of the Riders Quadrant. Sweet, sharp, and sneakily strong, like the cadets drinking it, this cocktail doesn't ask permission. It announces its presence, loud and lovely.

HONEY LAVENDER SIMPLE SYRUP

1 cup (240 ml) water

1 cup (320 g) honey

2 tablespoons (3.5 g) dried culinary-grade lavender buds

HONEY LAVENDER LEMONADE

2 cups (475 ml) freshly squeezed lemon juice (from 8 large lemons)

5 cups (1.2 L) water

FOR EACH COCKTAIL

Ice, for serving

1 cup (240 ml) honey lavender lemonade

2 ounces (60 ml) Empress 1908 gin

Lemon slice, for garnish

Fresh organic lavender sprig, for garnish

To make the honey lavender simple syrup: In a small saucepan over medium-low heat, bring the water to a simmer. Remove from the heat and stir in the honey until dissolved fully. Add the lavender buds, cover, and let steep for 30 minutes or up to 2 hours. Strain through a fine-mesh sieve into a bowl or jar, discarding the solids. Use immediately, or store in an airtight container in the refrigerator for up to 1 month.

To make the honey lavender lemonade: In a large pitcher, combine the honey lavender simple syrup, lemon juice, and water. Stir well and refrigerate until chilled.

To make each cocktail: Fill a glass (240 to 350 ml) with ice. Pour in the honey lavender lemonade and gin. Stir gently to combine. Garnish with a lemon slice and lavender sprig.

Store leftover lemonade in an airtight container in the refrigerator for up to 1 week.

YIELDS
8 SERVINGS

ICED
ARINMINT TEA

This iced tea is a tribute to Tyrrendor's most duplicitous herb: arinmint. With cooling mint layered over grassy green tea and balanced by honey and lemon, it's as refreshing as it is deceptive. Steeped for its gentle healing properties, arinmint is beloved across the wards—just don't pair it with the wrong bark, or you'll be counting down to your last breath. Served over ice with a splash of sparkling water and a slice of caution, this drink is best enjoyed in good company . . . and with complete trust in whoever's pouring.

8 cups (1.9 L) water

3 tablespoons (6 g) loose green-tea leaves, or 8 green tea bags

½ cup (12 g) fresh mint leaves, plus more for garnish (optional)

⅓ cup (107 g) honey, or to taste

½ cup (120 ml) freshly squeezed lemon juice (from 2 large lemons)

Ice, for serving

Sparkling water, for topping

In a medium saucepan, bring the water to a boil over high heat. Remove the pot from heat and add the tea leaves and mint. Cover and steep for 10 minutes. Strain the tea through a fine-mesh sieve into a large pitcher. Discard the solids.

Stir in the honey and lemon juice. Refrigerate until well chilled.

To serve, fill a glass with ice, pour in the tea, leaving a bit of room, and top with sparkling water. Give it a quick stir to combine and garnish with fresh mint, if desired.

YIELDS
6 TO 8 SERVINGS

"KILL YOU IN A GOWN" CHAMPAGNE GRANITA

There's dressed to kill, and then there's Mira Sorrengail. Cool under pressure and deadly even in heels, she delivers one of the most cutting lines in Iron Flame *with the same poise she brings to every battlefield, be it blood soaked or velvet draped. This sparkling granita channels that energy: elegant, ice-cold, and laced with danger. With crisp Champagne, a whisper of spiced rose syrup, and a garnish of rosebud, it's the perfect palate cleanser for anyone who's ever made an entrance while ready to kill. Serve in a coupe. Don't underestimate the woman holding it.*

ROSE SIMPLE SYRUP

½ cup (120 ml) water

½ cup (120 ml) rose water

1 cup (200 g) granulated sugar

½ teaspoon (1.3 g) ground cinnamon

GRANITA

One 750 ml bottle Champagne or sparkling white wine, chilled

Grated zest and juice of 2 lemons

Organic rosebuds, for garnish (optional)

To make the rose simple syrup: In a small saucepan over medium heat, combine the water, rose water, sugar, and cinnamon. Cook, stirring, until the sugar dissolves completely, 2 to 3 minutes. Remove from the heat and let cool to room temperature.

To make the granita: In a 9-by-12-inch (23 by 30 cm) metal pan or glass baking dish, combine the rose simple syrup, chilled Champagne, lemon juice, and lemon zest. Stir gently to combine. Place the dish in the freezer for 30 minutes.

After 30 minutes, use a fork or wooden spoon to scrape any ice crystals from the edges and mix them into the center. Repeat freezing and scraping every 30 to 60 minutes for 3 to 4 hours, or until the mixture has a fluffy, granular texture.

Before serving, use a fork to fluff the granita. Spoon into coupe glasses or small bowls. Garnish each serving with a rosebud, if desired, and serve immediately.

JESINIA'S MARGIN NOTES

The Rose Simple Syrup can be made ahead and stored in an airtight container in the refrigerator for up to 1 month.

YIELDS 1 COCKTAIL, PLUS EXTRA SYRUP

THE AMBER PAINKILLER

"Drink this," Winifred says, pulling a small vial from her belt after Imogen annihilates Violet's shoulder. Violet doesn't ask what it is, she just downs it. And thank the gods, because whatever that amber liquid is, it works. This cocktail may not be made by a mender, but it'll take the edge off. Bourbon-forward, with bruised peaches, ginger, honey, and just enough lemon, it's strong medicine with better taste.

PEACH HONEY SIMPLE SYRUP

1 cup (240 ml) water

1 cup (320 g) honey

1 large peach, sliced, about 1 cup (170 g)

FOR EACH COCKTAIL

Ice, for serving

2 ounces (60 ml) bourbon

½ ounce (15 ml) peach honey simple syrup

½ ounce (15 ml) freshly squeezed lemon juice

½ ounce (15 ml) ginger juice

Peach slice, for garnish

To make the peach honey simple syrup: In a small saucepan over medium-low heat, bring the water to a simmer. Remove from the heat and stir in the honey until dissolved fully. Add the peach slices and bruise them gently with a wooden spoon to release their juices. Cover and let steep for 15 minutes. Strain through a fine-mesh sieve into a bowl or jar and discard the solids. Refrigerate leftover syrup in an airtight container for up to 1 month.

To make each cocktail: Fill a rocks glass with ice. Pour in the bourbon, peach honey simple syrup, lemon juice, and ginger juice. Stir to combine. Garnish with a peach slice and serve immediately.

YIELDS
6 TO 8 SERVINGS

SIGNET DULLING CIDER

It smells like apple juice, but don't be fooled. In Iron Flame, *this concoction is anything but sweet. Forced on riders to sever their connections and dull their signets, it's a violation in a glass. This cocktail channels that unnerving disconnect: clean and apple-forward on the nose, then finished with a quiet burn that leaves you wondering what just slipped past your defenses.*

- 4 cups (950 ml) apple cider
- ½ cup (120 ml) apple brandy
- ½ cup (120 ml) bourbon
- ¼ cup (60 ml) freshly squeezed lemon juice
- ½ ounce (15 ml) lemon bitters
- Ice, for serving
- Green apple slices, for garnish

In a large pitcher, combine the apple cider, apple brandy, bourbon, lemon juice, and lemon bitters. Stir to combine and refrigerate until chilled.

To serve, fill a glass (240 to 350 ml) to the brim with ice. Pour the cocktail over the ice and garnish with a green apple slice. Serve cold.

YIELDS
8 SERVINGS

ISLES OF
RECKONING MANGO PUNCH

There's no easy path to truth, or to Irid dragons. As Violet and her squad hop from isle to isle in Onyx Storm, *they face blood trials, riddles, and roulette-like gifts. This punch is a tribute to that journey: tropical mango for Deverelli's beaches, lime and salt for Unnbriel's severity, and a kiss of cinnamon for the cunning warmth of Hedotis. Dark rum pulls it all together because, to find what you're looking for, sometimes you have to go through all five Isles and a hangover. (If you don't have simple syrup on hand, simply simmer equal parts sugar and water until clear.) Serve chilled and in large pitchers. Daggers optional.*

- 3 cups (700 ml) mango juice
- 2 cups (475 ml) pineapple juice
- 1½ cups (350 ml) barista-style coconut milk (from a carton, not canned)
- 1½ cups (350 ml) dark rum
- ½ cup (120 ml) freshly squeezed lime juice
- ½ cup (120 ml) triple sec
- ½ cup (120 ml) simple syrup
- 1 cinnamon stick
- 2 tablespoons (25 g) granulated sugar
- ¼ teaspoon (0.6 g) ground cinnamon
- 2 limes, cut into 8 wedges
- Ice, for serving

In a large pitcher, combine the mango juice, pineapple juice, coconut milk, rum, lime juice, triple sec, and simple syrup. Stir well to combine. Add the cinnamon stick. Refrigerate for at least 30 minutes, or up to overnight, to let the flavors deepen.

When ready to serve, on a small plate, mix the sugar and ground cinnamon. Run a lime wedge around the rim of 1 pint (475 ml) Mason jar or highball glass, then dip half the rim into the cinnamon-sugar mixture.

Fill the glass with ice and pour the punch into the glass. Garnish with the lime wedge. Serve immediately.

YIELDS
1 COCKTAIL

THE CLIFFHANGER
SPICED ESPRESSO MARTINI

This one's for the readers who turned the final page and screamed into the void. A bold espresso martini laced with warming spice and just enough sweetness to lull you into a false sense of peace. Much like an author we know and love, it delivers a jolt right at the very end. Shake it up, sip it slowly, and whatever you do, don't get too comfortable.

Ice, for shaking

1½ ounces (45 ml) vodka

1½ ounces (45 ml) cold-brew coffee concentrate

1 ounce (30 ml) coffee liqueur

¼ teaspoon (0.6 g) ground cinnamon

⅛ teaspoon (0.5 g) ground ginger

⅛ teaspoon (0.40 g) ground cardamom

3 coffee beans, for garnish

Fill a cocktail shaker with ice. Pour in the vodka, cold brew, and coffee liqueur. Add the cinnamon, ginger, and cardamom. Cover and shake vigorously until the shaker is frosty and the drink is well chilled, 15 to 30 seconds. Strain into a martini glass.

Garnish with the coffee beans and serve immediately.

YIELDS
1 COCKTAIL

SGAEYL'S SPRITZ

If dragons drank wine, Sgaeyl would sip a bone-dry Chardonnay from a crystal coupe with a talon casually curled, casting withering glances across the flight field. Elegant, lethal, and far above your nonsense, this spritz is her in liquid form: crisp and floral with a bite of lemon and a hit of elderflower that lingers longer than her patience. It's refined, sharp, and just effervescent enough to catch you off guard. Serve chilled, preferably while brooding, judging, or verbally eviscerating your enemies.

Ice, for serving

3 ounces (90 ml) chilled Chardonnay

1½ ounces (45 ml) St-Germain elderflower liqueur

½ ounce (15 ml) freshly squeezed lemon juice

1 ounce (30 ml) chilled club soda

Lemon wheel or twist, for garnish

Fill a large wineglass with ice. Pour in the Chardonnay, St-Germain, and lemon juice. Stir to combine and chill. Top with the club soda and stir gently to incorporate.

Garnish with a lemon wheel. Serve immediately.

8

MENUS FOR MAYHEM AND MERRIMENT

Cadets gathering for non-sanctioned meals, celebrations, or social engagements may be subject to disciplinary review. Exceptions may be granted in cases of memorial feasts, post-victory events, or if the commandant is not informed.

—Addendum 7.1, The Basgiath War College Code of Conduct

This isn't just a recipe book—it's an invitation to experience the series in a whole new way.

What follows is a collection of party menus built for squad dinners, late-night scream sessions, Gauntlet Eve carbo loads, and the kind of toasts that happen when no one knows if tomorrow's coming. Whether you're hosting a book club, a formal dinner with friends, or a brunch where the dress code is "post-survival," these themed gatherings let you bring the world of *Fourth Wing* to your table.

Use them as written or build your own. We won't report you.

MAT CHALLENGE
WATCH PARTY

Grab a seat (but don't get too comfortable) and prepare to cheer, cringe, and maybe place a few reckless bets as your favorite cadets take to the mat. Whether you're watching your friends throw down or just queuing up the next episode of your favorite series, this casual gathering is all about snacks and even snarky commentary.

This is the ultimate low-stakes, high-sass party, perfect for weeknights, roommate hangs, or impromptu rewatch sessions. Keep it chill, but don't skimp on the competition: You can always turn the night into a trivia battle or board-game night.

Vibe: Competitive but cozy—think throw pillows on the floor, camp chairs pulled up to the screen, and everyone talking over each other.

Dress Code: Athleisure, obviously. Bonus points for anyone who shows up in their leathers.

Décor: Tape down a "mat" in the middle of the room and hang some parchment-style brackets.

Game Idea: Pull out your favorite card or board game, something that's well suited to a bracket-style competition.

What to Bring: A competitive spirit, your loudest commentary voice, and something ice-cold for the victor.

MENU

Basgiath Lavender Lemonade
PAGE 132

"Don't Die" Nachos
PAGE 52

Popcorn Conduits
PAGE 44

Rider's Ration Feta Flatbread
PAGE 65

Violent Little Kebabs
PAGE 72

Scorched Earth S'mores Bars
PAGE 128

A "BLADES BENEATH THE TABLE" FEAST

The best feasts aren't always the friendliest. Inspired by the tense, tactical meals shared in The Empyrean series, where alliances are tested, smiles are sharpened, and every compliment might carry a threat, this menu is meant for gatherings where charm and strategy go hand in hand.

Ideal for dinner parties with your most cunning friends, this feast balances elegance and edge: bold flavors, artful presentation, and just enough sweetness to lower defenses.

Vibe: Formal(-ish) but fraught. Candles burn low, side glances are exchanged, and someone's definitely hiding something.

Dress Code: Think court intrigue. Dark linens, sharp tailoring, and jewelry that could double as a weapon.

Décor: Long table, black taper candles, place cards with veiled threats or false titles.

Game Idea: "Lie to Me"—everyone writes one true and one false detail about themselves on cards. Guests guess the lie. Bonus if you do it in character.

What to Bring: Your most disarming smile and a bottle you wouldn't mind poisoning (if all else fails).

MENU

"Kill You in a Gown" Champagne Granita
PAGE 136

Sorrengail's Secrets Stuffed Dates
PAGE 49

Diplomatic Roasted Chicken
PAGE 75

Vidirys Cauliflower Stuffing
PAGE 100

Xaden's Chocolate Cake
PAGE 110

GAUNTLET EVE CARBO LOAD

Only the unprepared face the Gauntlet on an empty stomach. Inspired by the eve of one of Basgiath's most brutal tests, this carb-forward spread is designed to fuel cadets before their climb, or maybe just friends before a long night of games, TV, or emotionally chaotic book talk.

This isn't a light snack situation. It's a full-on feast packed with comforting flavors and just enough spice to keep your pulse racing. Every dish represents a part of the infamous obstacle course, from the swinging chains to the near-vertical final climb. It's cheeky, over the top, and everything a cadet would want before risking their neck in the name of glory.

Vibe: Chaotic optimism. Nerves are high, portions are huge. Think prebattle banquet meets team-building pep talk.

Dress Code: Stretchy pants, or whatever you'd wear to carbo load like your life depends on it. Basically, whatever lets you eat lasagna without restriction.

Décor: Zigzagging table runners to mimic the ridgeline path, dangling "ropes" overhead if you're feeling ambitious.

Game Idea: Mini obstacle relay (paper toss, jumping jacks, blindfold spin, etc.) with a stopwatch to crown a Presentation Day Champion.

What to Bring: Your appetite, your best pep talk, and maybe a printed will (just in case).

MENU

The Cliffhanger Spiced Espresso Martini
PAGE 142

Spinning Garlic Parmesan Wheels
PAGE 96

Cheesy Buoy Ball Bites
PAGE 46

Shaking Pillar Veggie Skewers
PAGE 108

Rolling Log Lasagna
PAGE 89

Vertical Victory Brownie Trifle
PAGE 123

TRIAL BY FLAME
A GRILLED FEAST

This is a party for riders who don't flinch at a little smoke in the air or scorch on their plate. Whether you're celebrating a successful threshing, your own grilling prowess, or just the fact that it's not raining, this feast is all about fire-forged flavor.

Inspired by the Riders Quadrant's trial-by-flame attitude and the dragons who breathe life into the battlefield, this menu is built to be cooked outdoors (or at least to taste like it was). Char, sear, and a little chaos are encouraged. It's casual enough for a backyard hang, but bold enough for a midsummer solstice bash in the Vale.

Vibe: Smoke in your eyes and sauce on your fingers but with laughter that cuts the heat. Something is bound to get singed, but hopefully it's just the food.

Dress Code: Casual, sun worn, and flame-retardant wouldn't hurt.

Décor: Want a craft project? Make lanterns with dragon silhouettes. Bonus points for as many real flames as possible (torches, candles, firepits, etc.).

Game Idea: Host a "Flame Trial" blind taste-test of spicy condiments ranked by heat level. Last one standing wins bragging rights (and probably some milk).

What to Bring: Something cold to drink and courage to try the hottest thing on the table.

MENU

Iced Arinmint Tea
PAGE 135

Inferno Wings
PAGE 47

Scorched Herd Sliders
PAGE 84

Flame-Kissed Corn on the Cob
PAGE 101

Embered Potato Packets
PAGE 106

Dragonfire Peaches with Honey, Pistachios, and Ice Cream
PAGE 119

DAWN FORMATION BRUNCH

Some mornings hit harder than others, like the ones that start with a sunrise roll call or a hang-over from too many cups of Basgiath Lavender Lemonade (page 132). Whether you're fueling up for a day of flight drills or simply recovering, this brunch delivers everything you need: protein, pastry, and plausible deniability. It's also perfect for book clubs, weekend gatherings, or celebrating a friend who just made wingleader.

Vibe: This is the kind of morning that starts quiet and ends with plans for rebellion.

Dress Code: Pajamas or the comfiest sundress. Bonus points for braided hair.

Décor: Mismatched mugs, parchment-style place cards, just-picked and thrown-together flower bouquets.

Game Idea: "Who Said It?" brunch edition. Read quotes from the book and guess who said them—wrong answers require a sip of Isles of Reckoning Mango Punch.

What to Bring: Something baked, your opinions about plot twists, and just enough gossip to count as intel.

MENU

LUNCH DATE WITH XADEN AND VIOLET

Not all sparks fly on the battlefield. Sometimes they show up over charred soup and honest conversation (or well-written letters). This lunch is for lingering glances, slow bites, and a moment of quiet in a world that doesn't often allow for it. Whether you're sharing it with a partner, a best friend, or just enjoying the luxury of eating lunch while seated, this spread is simple, intentional, and tasty as hell . . . just like a certain marked wingleader.

Vibe: Intimate and unpretentious, think wind rustling your hair and a view of the Vale. Don't worry, a picnic in the park will suffice.

Dress Code: Whatever makes you feel confident. A sweater, worn leathers, or that shirt you stole from your squadmate.

Décor: A blanket under the open sky, linen napkins if you're feeling fancy. Likely a dragon keeping a respectful distance (physically, if not mentally).

Game Idea: "Truth or Dare, Basgiath Edition." No skipping. No lying. No shadow magic.

What to Bring: A blanket, a chilled bottle of white wine, and good conversation.

MENU

Basgiath Mess Hall Turkey Melt
PAGE 56

Lilith's Charred Tomato and Roasted Garlic Soup
PAGE 69

Riorson House Chopped Salad
PAGE 63

Andarna's Butterscotch Chocolate Eclipse Cookies
PAGE 127

ACKNOWLEDGMENTS

This book is dedicated to my daughter, Molly. My last cookbook, *A Feast of Thorns and Roses*, was dedicated to her brother, Reggie, so it only felt right. I wrote that book while he was a newborn, but I'm hoping this manuscript will be complete before Molly's arrival, while her brother has been running circles around my legs and serving as a less-than-helpful recipe tester (toddlers, amiright?). As I type this, recipe testing is nearly complete, and I'm about thirty-eight weeks pregnant. We can do this, Molly! My deepest thanks for keeping this pregnancy normal and boring so Mom could crank out some work. It's been so fun to develop this book with you as my little buddy, cheering me on while I sneak in work during the margins of the day and your brother's naptime. I love you so much, and I can't wait to meet you.

And Reggie, my sweet boy. You've taught me so much about myself. Namely, that I'm capable of more than I ever imagined. If I thought writing a cookbook with you as a newborn was hard, it was nothing compared to writing one with you as a toddler. It's so fun to watch your world grow, and as challenging as it can be to keep up, I'm grateful you're so eager to share it with me. You are the light of my world. I love you.

To Eric, my husband of nearly ten years and BFF for nineteen: Thank you for everything. Thank you for all your support as I've written four (four!) cookbooks now. Thank you for your unwavering encouragement and for being the best cheerleader. Thank you for tracking my sales, reviews, and rankings daily, and for being just as excited for my success as I am, if not more. Thank you for being the best dad to our kids and for giving me the breathing room I need to maintain a career while staying home with them. I love you.

Mom, I truly couldn't have done any of this without you. Grandma Wednesdays are the *best* day of the week, for both Reggie and me. We're so lucky to have you. Not only are you the best grandma and playmate, always willing to entertain when Mom needs time, you've also been endlessly supportive of my cookbook dreams and have gone above and beyond to help me make all my wild ideas happen. I'm so, so grateful for you and all the time you've sacrificed to support me. I love you.

Thank you to Sally Ekus, the world's best literary agent. I'm constantly in awe of you and everything you do. You've taught me so much and advocated for me so well. Thank you for being my partner in this.

Thank you to Edward, my editor, for being as excited about this project as I am and for helping bring this world to life in cookbook form. Working with you is always a wonderful experience.

Thank you to my Kitchen Quadrant, aka the amazing recipe testers who helped shape these recipes into what they are! I'm so grateful for your time and feedback, each and every one of you:

Laurie Miller

Tami Grabinski

Mara Kucirek (also my virtual assistant extraordinaire!)

Amanda French

Amanda Katz

Anna Page

Ann Baum

Arielle Jagow

Aryel Reed

Ashleigh Cosgriff

Ashley Roe

Becky Kistler

Brooke Kelley

Danielle Hardie

Ellen Stoll

Hannah Soileau

Holly Anders

Jen Williams

Jocelyn De La Rosa

Kayla Sullivan

Katrina White

Kelsey Imberg

Keri Waites

Lilly Nickels

Lindsey Alpert

Rachael Dent

Sam Bennett

Skylar Hatch

Sydney Victorson

And, finally, thank you to all the friends who let me bounce ideas off them—Ann, Jenn, Lauren, Kayla, Amy, and so many others. As you well know by now, I just can't work in a vacuum, and I so appreciate you!

INDEX

ABOUT THE AUTHOR

Chelsea Cole is a cookbook author and food blogger from Portland, Oregon. Her culinary journey began with her blog, *A Duck's Oven*, which she started during her time as a student at the University of Oregon. What began as a resource for students navigating the kitchen has grown into a decade-long exploration of sous vide cooking and family-friendly recipes.

Chelsea has authored four cookbooks: *Everyday Sous Vide* and *Sous Vide Meal Prep*, which demystify the technique for home cooks, and *A Feast of Thorns and Roses* and *A Guide to the Kitchen Quadrant*, which bring the fantastical food from beloved fantasy series to the tables of fans everywhere.

Alongside her professional pursuits, Chelsea spends her days wrangling two kids with her husband outside of Portland, Oregon. Whether she's exploring the city's culinary scene, camping, or learning to make cheese, she's always on a mission to inspire others to get in the kitchen and try something new.

weldon**owen**
an imprint of Insight Editions
P.O. Box 3088
San Rafael, CA 94912
www.weldonowen.com

CEO Raoul Goff
SVP Group Publisher Jeff McLaughlin
VP Publisher Roger Shaw
Associate Publisher Thom O'Hearn
Executive Editor Edward Ash-Milby
Assistant Editor Kayla Belser
Managing Editor Michelle Hope
Production Editor Ivy Long
Art Director and Designer Megan Sinead Bingham
Production Designer Jean Hwang
VP Manufacturing Alix Nicholaeff
Senior Production Manager Joshua Smith
Strategic Production Planner Lina s Palma-Temena

Photography and Propping Waterbury Publications
Food Styling Joshua Hake

Weldon Owen would also like to thank Mary Cassells and Sharon Silva.

ISBN: 979-8-88674-404-0

Manufactured in China by Insight Editions
10 9 8 7 6 5 4 3 2 1

ROOTS of PEACE REPLANTED PAPER

Insight Editions, in association with Roots of Peace, will plant two trees for each tree used in the manufacturing of this book. Roots of Peace is an internationally renowned humanitarian organization dedicated to eradicating land mines worldwide and converting war-torn lands into productive farms and wildlife habitats. Roots of Peace will plant two million fruit and nut trees in Afghanistan and provide farmers there with the skills and support necessary for sustainable land use.